Steve
Chandler

FEARLESS

Creating the Courage to
Change the Things You Can

Robert D. Reed Publishers • Bandon, OR

Robert D. Reed Publishers
P.O. Box 1992
Bandon, OR 97411
Phone: 541-347-9882 • Fax: -9883
E-mail: 4bobreed@msn.com
web site: www.rdrpublishers.com

Cover Designer: **Cleone Lyvonne**
Editor: **Kathy Chandler**
Typesetter: **Barbara Kruger**

Cover Photo: *In Jeopardy,* © Marting, from dreamstime.com

ISBN: 978-1-934759-15-8
ISBN 10: 1-934759-15-5

Library of Congress Control Number 2008928851

Manufactured, typeset and printed in the United States of America

To Steve Hardison

Don't cure me. Sickness is my me.
My terror was you'd set me free.

Frederick Seidel

Contents

Contents *(continued)*

Acknowledgments

To Steve Hardison for the ultimate experience in coaching.

To Kathy Chandler for editing and guidance all along the way.

To Byron Katie for the school and the work and the great undoing.

To Maurice Bassett and Julie Blake for their tireless contributions to the MindShift project.

To Angela Hardison for the art and beauty.

To Sam Beckford and the members of the Creators Landing event.

To Bob Reed and Cleone for publishing miracles.

People say we got it made.
Don't they know we're so afraid?

John Lennon
Isolation

Chapter 1

They say never push a coward

They say never push a coward.

They say if you push a coward far enough, he will snap like no other. Like no brave man will snap. Push a brave man, and the brave man will push back. He won't allow himself to be pushed.

Push a coward and he won't push back. Push him more, and he'll still take it. But push him too far . . . well, then you have to watch out.

Because a coward will come back out the other side. He won't just be a brave guy; he'll be insane. You'll be introduced to a wild animal.

I'm a coward myself.

Chapter 2

Searching for the courage code

My work as a coach and trainer gives me opportunities to study courage and cowardice at close range. Success begins with desire. People all desire success but they don't always know how to achieve it.

When I work with you on the subject of success, I begin with the question: "What would you like to create?" And once you can identify that for me, my second question is "What's in the way of that right now?"

As if I didn't know.

Because it's always the same thing. Even though I've had it described to me a thousand different ways. It's the same thing. It's not money or circumstance or time. It's fear. Fear is all that's in your way.

"I'm afraid if I did my dream, I would lose my security. I'm afraid my family wouldn't understand it if I did this. I'm afraid I don't know *how* to do it. I'm afraid I won't have time."

Those were my words, too! Most of my life I wrestled with these same fears. My own cowardice stopped me. I've written about this before. Courage has been my obsession because of my lack of it. Even as a little boy I remember that I always longed to be Mighty Mouse, then popular on TV cartoons and in comic books. It was becoming clear to me when I was young that I had no super powers myself. There was sadness and pain and large doses of fear around such threats as wild animals and bullies. So watching heroes like Mighty Mouse and, later, Superman, lit my little boy's heart right up.

Things would go wrong and people would be in danger and just when you thought things couldn't get worse, Mighty Mouse would *fly in* singing, "Here I come to save the day!" Even today, when I see a picture of Mighty Mouse, I feel a little shiver of good feelings.

Later, as I collected comic books, I also became a fan of Atomic Mouse. Atomic Mouse had no superpowers until he took his U235 pill! I always wondered if my later addictions could be traced back to Atomic Mouse . . . one pill and he was invincible!

It could be that my whole life has been a search for superpowers. So I could fly. And if a bully ever struck I would feel nothing. Most of my life I felt like someone searching the world for a secret . . . a secret code to break so that courage would be available.

I remember once—many years ago—bragging to friends in a bar in New York that I was going to write a book called *The Courage Prayer*. But I didn't believe it for a minute. Not down deep. Fear was in my way.

I had gotten the idea for that title while I was going through recovery from addiction. While going to meetings, I was frustrated by this prayer we all recited called The Serenity Prayer. Serenity? Who needed serenity? I thought, this isn't a nursing home; this is re-entry into life. The prayer said, "God, grant me the serenity to accept the things I cannot change, the courage to change the things I can, and the wisdom to know the difference."

I always secretly called that prayer "the courage prayer." What I wanted from that prayer was the courage. The courage to change the things I could. How would that be? Forget serenity. At least for now. That could come later when I was enjoying the benefits of elderly living.

Courage is all any of my clients have ever wanted, too. Though they call it a million different things. Courage is always what is missing. (For example, even the solution to the time management problem is the introduction of *boldness*.) In all quests for success, what people really want to be is fearless.

So I'll tell you how I get them there.

Life shrinks or expands
in proportion to one's courage.

Anais Nin

Chapter 3

Death is like the rose

I was sitting in Byron Katie's nine-day school and we were about to go on a field trip to conduct some very brave experiments. Many of us, including me, were scared. As we were about to board the buses Katie said to all 300 of us, "Remember, the worst thing that could happen to you is a thought."

I burst out laughing! It wasn't the first time I laughed or cried in that school. But the laughs were always joyful and the crying was sweet and grateful. Like crying at a wedding. Finally experiencing the marriage of mind and spirit.

Of life and death.

I'd been listening to Katie for a few years prior to the school on audio recordings played in my car as I drove around or in my headphones as I drifted off to sleep at night. She said one night, as I was falling into a dream state, that if she were to throw me out of an airplane without a parachute the worst thing that could happen to me all the way down was a thought. I slept well that night.

Our fear of death is staggering. Sometimes I think if we could simply erase *that* fear, everything would be okay.

Death even causes us to fear how our bodies change as they get older. We judge the body's changes to be a bad thing. Yet the rose I bought you fades and dies beautifully. You save it, even. You thumbtack it above our bed. It is dry now, and even what some might call dead. But it looks so beautiful and natural.

All form changes. All pain comes from fear of that. Fearless is the rose that fades and dries and falls from the wall, beautiful all the way down.

Some say that *all* fear is fear of death. But why do we fear death? Do we fear sleep? Deep, peaceful dreamless sleep? Where does the world go when I disappear into dreamless sleep? Why am I not anxious about going to sleep and losing everything there? After all, a day is ending . . . a day that is always my life in microcosm. Asleep now, I am happily "dead to the world," and feeling no hint of trouble as I lie fearless beneath the faded red rose pinned above the head of the bed.

You have done a good thing by putting the rose up to die so beautifully right before our eyes.

If you realize that all things change,
there is nothing you will try
to hold on to.
If you aren't afraid of dying,
there is nothing you can't achieve.

Lao Tzu

Chapter 4

Our life will never end

To understand the elimination of fear from my life, I must appreciate the role of thought. Because every feeling—especially fear—begins with a thought. And every thought causes a feeling. Nothing else can cause a feeling. Let me give you a very gentle example to begin with. Then we'll crank it up later.

In most of the world, and in Michigan where I grew up, rain was a metaphor for sadness and pain. Our whole society seemed to regard it this way. Into every life a little rain must fall. George and Martha have a "stormy" relationship. Rain is sorrow.

But sunshine! Sunshine is good . . . rain bad, sun good . . . you are the sunshine of my life. Things going badly? Don't worry. Here comes the sun! And it's all right.

The secret to bad and good and love and fear is reflected in our views of rain. How we interpret the rain. In Arizona, for example, we don't think the rain is so bad because weather itself is not a concept that we are overly familiar with. When clouds appear, we start feeling romantic. When we watch a movie mystery set in rainy, foggy London town, we wish we were there.

Driving to Tucson recently the romance of the rain did not let us down. The winds blew across the desert, and as we looked out toward the Catalina Mountains black clouds crackled with thunder and lightning. Rain fell. We smiled and walked slowly from our car to go meet our friends Fred and Lynette.

Fred is Fred Knipe—someone I met in Tucson at college in 1964. Later the two of us wrote songs together for a living for a number of years. Three of our songs had the word "rain" in the title. ("Rain on Me," "Rain Forest" and "Melinda Rain.") In each of those songs, the element of rain was a positive *romantic* element. Most songwriters write songs wherein the rain is a negative thing: "Stormy Weather," "Baby, The Rain Must Fall" and "I Made It Through the Rain" are examples.

But it's all perception. Every feeling in life is! Perceive something one way and you are terrified. Perceive it another way, and you are happy. You yourself get to write the perception. Always in life, *you* get to compose the song.

Consider the eerie power of Jim Morrison singing "Riders on the Storm." ("The world on you depends/ Our life will never end.") You hear rain behind the opening cascading keyboards as Morrison sings of the storm and how it brings out the dark side of humanity, a killer on the road; his brain is "squirming like a toad."

But without his interpretation, the rain means nothing.

I actually saw a little toad come out of the desert last night. I wasn't thinking like Morrison at the time, so I decided it was good. The toad hopped across my path and enjoyed moving along the rain-slick patio tiles at the resort. He had suction-cups for feet. I smiled at the sight of him. Rain is a thought that is welcome here. All sad things can be beautiful when the mind is right. Fear is washed away in the blink of an eye. In the turning of a thought fear is washed away.

Chapter 5

Life's most troubling comic material

I saw Robin Williams on *Inside the Actor's Studio* once and he stood up and asked the audience to throw an object—any object, anything—up to the stage.

Someone threw him a towel.

He wrapped it around his head and took on a foreign accent and said some hilarious things—then he put it around his waist and acted like a delicate man at a steam bath—people roared, although the towel was just any object—a neutral, meaningless thing until he used it. Re-interpreted it. Just as we do with all the troubling comic material of our private lives.

My coach uses my problem the same way. To him it is "material." He creates with it. He twists it around into different shapes. By the time we are finished, we are both glad the problem is here because we have taken so much from it. My coach (yes, he's a real person, www.theultimatecoach.net) Steve Hardison says, "This 'problem' is going to be a great seminar for you. You couldn't have invented a better seminar for you to take right now."

Solutions are one of the great joys of the fearless life. And all solutions have problems. You can't have a solution without a problem, and a life without solutions is flat and boring. Some coaches and mentors know how to use problems to create solutions so elegant that it would make Einstein jealous.

That's the fascinating thing about problems. When taken on, they are life-changing gifts. Once we can do the mind shift (from paranoid mode to creative mode) necessary to see them for what they are, all problems become advanced seminars in What I Now Need to Learn to Advance on this Spiritual Journey Up the Ladder of Consciousness to Some Real Fun and Good Mischief and a condition we've all heard described as fearless.

Chapter 6

Your kids have turned out great!

My seminar attendee in Boulder was named Tracy. She was in the process of outlining her financial desires and describing a good business plan when she blurted out, "But most of the men in here won't understand this, because I am a single mom and I have a child to raise. I do have a son."

Some men, because they have imaginations, *can* understand her. Compassion does not come from having experienced someone's identical life experience. Compassion comes from imagination.

I myself understood that woman's fear, both because I could imagine it—and also because I was a single father myself raising four young children on my own. I had full custody of those kids while also having my own business to run, and so I do have compassion for what single mothers experience. I was one! In fact now that I think of it my children back then would even sometimes *refer* to me as a "mother."

What a gift to me that time was. What a joy to have that experience, no matter how wild it was. My children and I used to watch the movie *Meatballs* to absorb the central message that "It just doesn't matter." Whatever our situation was at home, it didn't matter. Not even a little bit. Everything "negative" was illusory, and everything good felt real. There was enough love, music and humor to cover for us. We covered the spread. We knew we had nothing to fear from the rich kids in the camp across the lake.

Was I a good father? No one will ever know. Was I fearful about how my children would "turn out?" No. Not at all. They were not muffins. They were not in an oven. They were free spirits. There would be no "turning out" one way or the other because they were never going to get that final evaluation.

Most parents are always checking in the oven to see if the kids are turning out okay.

"I hope he turns out okay."

What is okay? What exactly do you want from him? Where does this fear come from? Will you be graded on how he turns out? That's really it, isn't it? It's a concern about *you*, isn't it?

My daughter Margie told me a story recently I hadn't remembered. She was in grade school, and it was her birthday. Her favorite color was always purple. And as she came outside for recess that one birthday day she saw me sitting on a swing in the playground with a large bouquet of purple flowers in my arms. I had no fear about how she would turn out. I just wanted to celebrate how perfect she already always was.

Chapter 7

Time is never disappearing

A lot of fear arises when we think about disappearing time. The sand running out of the hourglass. It feels like there's never enough time. It feels like that, anyway.

But while feeling that way you miss something. You miss the secret truth (and therefore beauty) beneath this gathering storm of unfinished tasks: you have all the time in the world. You have nothing *but* time. Time sweet time will remain infinite for you, always abundant, yet always just this moment right now.

Time is what being alive is made of. If you'll slow down you'll feel it. You'll feel all the time in the world right now.

And yet people sit with their friends and say, "I don't have time." Not realizing that time is *all* they have.

If I think I am upset *because* of my unfinished tasks, I have a chance to see my mind at play. Because I'm not really upset because of these tasks. I am upset because of the *thoughts* I believe about them.

When people think their problem is time management, it is not. Time itself cannot be managed. The problem here is boldness. The problem is the courage to say *no* to the things that distract your simplest journey.

When I'm upset, I'm upset by thoughts (just passing thoughts) about how my life *should be* versus how it really is.

How life really *is* is Robin Williams's towel. It's material for the act. The whole world is a stage and we all play a part. Fate had me playing in love with you as my sweetheart. Act one was when we met.

If the activity is important enough (falling in love with you), time is not an issue. So the secret to a fearless relationship with time is for me to slow down and focus. Focus fully on the one thing, the only thing.

Courage is not the absence of fear,
but rather the judgment
that something else
is more important than fear.

Ambrose Redmoon

Chapter 8

How about a business run by a child?

My client Curt has a seminar business and he employs seven people. He tries to please his people day-in-day-out but once the business enters the panic stage (because his people aren't performing) he blows up. Or else he melts down. (For variation.)

Curt is a typical reactor. My work as his consultant is to help him convert himself into a creator. To grow him up, like my coach did for me. That's when his business will thrive. And that's when his people will respect him.

For people to succeed in the world of business it sometimes helps to have them re-enter the world of art. Did you paint things as a little kid? Then you qualify. In one of the most no-nonsense competitive challenges in the world—coaching college basketball—the most successful coach of all time found the formula for his success from the world of art. John Wooden of UCLA said his formula was to "Make each day your masterpiece."

We know who Van Gogh is and who Leonardo DaVinci is, but what, exactly, constitutes a masterpiece? What day can you recall recently that you would call a masterpiece?

Most people would not be able to recall such a day. Simply because they don't create their days that way. They aren't producing a work of art. They're reacting to fears . . .

underlying and outright fears about what other people are doing and thinking. That's what makes up each day . . . a reaction to fears. I'm torn up inside about what other people are now thinking. Are they thinking I owe them money and can't be trusted? Are they thinking I'm not a good provider? Are they thinking I'm not good at what I do? I now scramble to try (in vain) to change those perceptions.

Most people are "trained" in childhood to react to their fears of other people. First try to please. Then react. Everyone else is in charge of your life.

Curt had had it with his people. And they with him! His employees were tired of trying to anticipate his meltdowns and blow ups. It's hard to run a successful team on stress. As if stress could become your motivator.

"What do you want to create?" I asked him. But it wasn't a question he was comfortable with. People like Curt would rather be upset. He would rather make other people wrong, be fed up, then find other stressed-out people to commiserate with. Because it's all he knows. The thought of *creativity* causes discomfort in him.

But Curt hung in there with me and decided to create a team. He wanted to build a team that produced dependable, ongoing profit for his business. So he began designing innovative communication systems that would guarantee that. He then tied his people's compensation to the month's profit and by so doing changed everyone's thinking! A game had begun.

Now, here is where business owners will want to stop me. Here is where I will hear from them! A thousand emails! They'll ask me for Curt's exact systems. They'll want techniques and tips; but that's just where they will go south. So I won't reveal them. These tips wouldn't work for them anyway! They were Curt's creations, designed to fit Curt's world.

Besides, tips and techniques are not what's missing. *Knowledge* of how to succeed is never what's missing. Remember my question to Curt? What do you *want to* create? What's missing is the *want to*. Total fearless committed responsibility for producing an outcome! And that's the secret formula.

This works for you, too. The courage to create means that you *yourself* will create systems that guarantee your own success based on how much they serve your people.

Curt's business is exciting now. And every time it veers off course it's because he is reacting and not creating. My only job on the coaching calendar is to continuously return him to the act of creation. How do I do this?

I ask him what he wants.

This is what you were born with

Every human is born with a creative drive. You were. And as a child you expressed it every day. When someone brought out the crayons you weren't frozen with fear, you eagerly filled the page with color.

When you played you made up stories freely. You didn't worry whether you were a published playwright. You made stories up. Then you sang. You danced around, without having been taught to dance. In the sand you built a castle, even though you had not been certified as an architect. What were you thinking? You weren't.

You were creating, from the right brain . . . nonlinear picture-making. Versus reacting. The ultimate choice that gets you back to courage.

I get my Scrabble tiles out so I can see once again how graphically the two words—creating and reacting—have the same letters in them. I spell the word R, E, A, C, T, I, N, G, and now rearrange the same letters and spell C, R, E, A, T, I, N, G. When you rearrange what Hercule Poirot called your "little grey cells" you, too, will go from reacting to creating.

For example, let's say I have 280 "important" emails from clients and colleagues and friends. (This happened just days ago.)

My usual unconscious "choice" is to react to that—a big sigh . . . I get up from my chair and take a walk around the grounds. Maybe even a drive to the post office to get my mind off the 280. Distraction! A little TV when I get home to check on the latest political developments. I'm a good citizen. I'm just keeping up. (No, I'm still reacting. To those emails. To the perceived overwhelm.)

Overwhelm is just a thought. It has no objective reality. So therefore it's time to shift. How can I find the gear called creating? I take a sheet of paper and put 28 empty boxes on it, each one representing 10 emails. The game is to fill all the little boxes. I put numbers in the boxes from one to 28, randomly distributed. I start replying to emails for about 20 minutes. Then I take my colored marker and fill in the squares, one square for every ten emails answered. I fill those in and look at my checkerboard. I like it that three squares are now filled in! It looks like I've made a good start, and it's fun, like a game.

Because it is a game. It's a created game. So it's my creation. And I can feel the shift. I'm no longer reacting to the overwhelm. I'm happily lost in the funhouse. My associate comes in and sees me blocking out squares in my checkerboard with my tongue out like a little kid coloring. She wonders when I'll get back to work.

Well I *would* go back to work if that would be effective. But games move life forward faster and they also give us a lot more energy. People do things on the playing field they would never have done in real life. Observers who cheer people on the playing field see a certain fearlessness they would not normally see in real life.

To live in the world of creation—to get into it and stay in it—to frequent it and haunt it ... to think intently and fruitfully, to woo combinations and inspirations into being by a depth and continuity of attention and meditation—this is the only thing.

Henry James

Chapter 10

What makes you so afraid?

So what are you thinking that makes you so afraid? (Because it's always what you're thinking. It's never the situation itself.)

"Well, I'm thinking I could go out of business . . . "

Well, OK, you *could* go out of business. Are you thinking you are *likely* to go out of business?

"Let me think about that. Well. Probably not likely. Not yet."

All right, it's good to identify that you're not likely to go out of business. We're starting to dissolve this thing called fear. We're starting to undo it.

But what if you *did* go out of business? Could you handle that? What would your life be like? Would your life be ruined forever? Is there a chance you could rebuild in another professional format that would be even stronger?

Because if you are really honest with the thought that is causing the fear, and you stay with it, and look at all the different variations and permutations of that particular thought, that thought loses its power. Because it loses its truth.

When you think, "I couldn't handle it if that happened," is that really true? You've handled everything so far. Everything life had to offer you have handled, in one way or another. So is it really true that you could not handle something in the future you're afraid will happen?

"Well, no, I just would be uncomfortable, though."

Good. Now we're getting somewhere. Because that's a different thought altogether! Notice the difference. If I'm walking around thinking, I'd be "uncomfortable" if something happened, I'm much less fearful than if I'm walking around thinking *I couldn't handle it* if that happened.

We think so many thoughts that are blown beyond reality by the dark habits of the imagination: "I would be devastated." "It would be huge." "I would die. I'd just die if that happened."

And notice how these thoughts get very dramatic and scary like a little kid's thoughts. It's the monster under the bed. Whenever something looks hard to do or even if we just don't have the final answers, these thoughts start to look up from under the bed. And the thoughts, when they're believed and clung to, then activate the trillions of cells in the body so that your biochemistry starts to poison the system and your heart starts to pound and the electromagnetic waves in the brain start to scramble like Israeli jets launched erratically from . . . a thought. From a single thought!—"I couldn't handle it if that happened."

Thoughts create fear. Thoughts create feelings. Yet most people don't experience it that way. Most people experience feelings being created by external events, and other people. And the future hiding under the bed.

So whenever I find a fear underneath something, I want to write the thought down behind that fear. I want to challenge the thought, and challenge it, and challenge it, as if I were an attorney in a very important case—challenging a witness. Because that thought is going to turn out to not be true. Try it and you'll find this out.

Chapter 11

Rachel was afraid of money

My friend is a rather well known author. I will call her Rachel so I can speak freely about some things that happened to her. First of all, Rachel was afraid of money.

Rachel was creative in many other areas of her life. She wrote inspiring, entertaining books. She had been a fashion model and was now a public speaker and a career consultant to people in the clothing industry. But about money she was not creative.

Rachel thought the whole act of selling her services was "tacky." When I asked her to tell me exactly how she viewed the thought of selling she said she pictured used car salespeople. Selling was a shady activity that she hated to participate in. (Rachel was, not surprisingly, making about a tenth of the money she could have been making if she hadn't felt this way.)

So Rachel wanted to hire me to teach her to make more money.

"You may have to lose your emotional attachments to money," I said.

"That's okay with me. I don't much like money," she said.

Which was a double bind for her because she now hated what she thought she needed. I explained how that was making her professional life not really work for her. (I could explain this clearly . . . not because I was superior to her in wisdom . . . but because I had been there myself. My money fears had been worse than hers.)

Rachel said, "Okay . . . I *need* money and I hate having to sell to get it."

And all that hating and needing added up to a huge emotional upset. I said to Rachel, "You are an emotional prisoner to money."

Rachel was not an isolated case. Most people are like Rachel. They don't have some rare untreatable disorder. They just have common human fear. Because they have strangely linked money to literal physical survival. It's a totally false link appearing true. It permeates the culture. Parents teach it to their children. It makes money seem like oxygen.

And we all know that lack of oxygen is terrifying. Ever get your ankle caught in seaweed deep underwater? Or this. Have you ever covered someone's mouth and nose and watch how they fight you to get their air back? Even a pacifist will fight you fiercely.

Imagine feeling that way about money.

If you associate money with breath and survival no wonder you feel the way you do when you think you have lost some. You panic. Or if you try to sell someone something and they are not interested! Oh my word they have rejected you. How does it feel to be a reject? A human reject. How does it feel to need a donor lung and not get it?

If you picture lost money you are disheartened, gloomy and "down," sometimes for days. It's like being denied life. "I don't want to buy your service" is like hearing from the doctor, "I'm afraid you don't have long to live." You are running out of oxygen!

The cure is this: Money must be repackaged, re-labeled, reconsidered and totally reconstituted in your mind to be a piece of paper. It's merely a piece of paper you use as a simple means of exchange. Money must go to neutral, like meaningless numbers in a friendly game. Money must now be about nothing but paper received for creativity and service.

From now on, no bad news about money. All news is neutral or good—good news can give you energy, so we don't want to eliminate that, although technically it's even better to have *all* money news be neutral. Are there ways to do this? We're getting there. But this very *concept* of neutral will help you immediately. Just to think it. It's the most important step. So let yourself perceive money as you do anything else: paint, rocks, paper, birds or grass.

Once you can do this, you are free. You can now focus on creating great things that serve others profoundly. Stay on that and money won't be a problem any more than paint and rocks are a problem. There's always enough. It's always unlimited. Focus on creating something masterful and you cannot be afraid. The two can't coexist.

Chapter 12

If I walked into your life today

How do we begin fearlessly creating good fortune from neutral? Well, let's look at the playing field and see what we are dealing with.

If I walked into your home office today, what would I find? I bet I would find other people's goals all over the place. I'd walk to your desk and see the utility company's written, specific goal on a piece of paper. I'd see the medical imaging center's goal for what they wanted to collect from you—down to the penny—in the next thirty days. I'd see your child's school's fundraising request to save the athletic program.

Other people's goals and dreams are all over *your place*. Written and definite. Guiding your life! Telling you what to do—how much money to make to meet *their* goals.

But where are yours? Your own goals? Where are they written down for you to see?

If we are guided by pieces of paper with numbers on them (and yes we are, all day long) why not create some of those numbers and papers ourselves? Why not make some that will benefit *us*? Why not just design them deliberately? Why not? Who's telling you not to?

You can actually create fearless numbers that will be yours. Written down. Posted where you can see them. Some of those numbers will go into your savings account. Others into a college fund, others to a vacation fund for a trip halfway around the world. Bold numbers. Fearless, actually. Because putting your own numbers up—ahead of other people's numbers—is also sometimes called *creating the courage to change the things you can.*

Start a huge, foolish project like Noah.
It makes absolutely no difference
what people think of you.

Rumi

Chapter 13

Hand me that appointment book

Now that I have walked through your home office pointing out how you are awash in other people's desires, it's time to hand me down my walking cane. I mean that. Hand me down my rockin' shoes, because I'm going to play it for you straight: without some additional changes you are going to *continue* to work each day for *other people's dreams*.

Even if you've put your own numbers up on the wall and on your mirror and over your desk. Even then! Don't believe me? Let's just look at your day planner.

Let's sit down and take a look. Open your day planner and show me what your days look like. That's it, wide open. So I can see it. Okay. I see many appointments. Tell me—one at a time—who they are with?

As we progress through your appointments I begin to notice something. Something interesting about your appointments. None of them are . . . well this is hard for me to say, so are you ready to hear this? . . . none of them are with *you*. They are all with other people.

It looks like *you* don't *rate*!

Because you don't have any time blocked out for yourself. No time to meet with yourself for your own planning. Or exercise. Or for meditation or contemplative prayer. No time in your planner for you to be in solitude. To just go alone into the silence so you can create. No appointment with the empty page. No breakfast meeting with your heart's desire. There's nothing here in your planner. No creative thinking time for yourself.

"I try to do all that stuff," my friend Arthur said, "exercise, meditation, planning . . . when I can work it in. If there's time left over."

Upside down, Arthur. Your life has capsized. It's now upside down. You are giving your most important activity (creating your life) the *least* attention and respect of all the things you do. Your own well-being is at the bottom of the list. Of all the people waiting to see you next week, you yourself are at the end of the line. You'll never meet with you because the line is too long.

I've delivered hundreds of seminars in my life but never yet the one I really wanted to deliver. What I want to do is put people in a room for a whole day with nothing but silence. Maybe have on the tables in front of them some blank pads of paper. It would be the ultimate seminar. A truly creative workshop.

We usually enter our highest state—our most creative state—in silence. But because so few of us design periods of solitude for ourselves we have no memory or experience of this. (Yet people will often innocently ask me, "Why do I get my best ideas when I'm in the shower?" Think it through! When else are you alone while awake?)

So because we have not scheduled any solitude or silence, we have to go to the second-most effective way to bring forth creativity: a crisis. When family members are seriously ill we are at our best. When things go horribly wrong, we rise up! We are at our most creative.

HR studies show that most people who get fired improve their lot in life whereas most people who quit do not. You'd think it would be the other way around. But people who are fired go into crisis mode. They wake up. They acquire a creative sense of urgency. They change their approach to life. They put *themselves* at the top of their appointment list: Priority Number One: Change My Life For The Better. Things get dramatically better. People who quit go through a long down time. Before crisis sets in and they finally rise back up.

But you can always rise up right now. Today. In solitude. And if you are a "busy" person, solitude itself will originally feel like a crisis. That's why it works. Soon the crisis mentality subsides, and in that solitude the best idea you've ever had emerges.

It takes courage to put yourself first. We've been shamed for being selfish. That was always the most cutting accusation. But when you start honoring your own time with yourself, you will still serve others. In fact even better. Because there's a more focused, masterful you to do the serving. So the difference is this: your own life comes first: a fearless decision.

Chapter 14

I went down the tubes really fast

Speaking of quitting, I remember quitting a job I had once. I went down the tubes really fast. I quit to go into business on my own and I didn't know how to run my own business. Taxes started accumulating unpaid. Soon mortgage payments were missed. And finally I was floundering around trying to sell people on me and win them over. Trying to win over my prospective clients. The crisis deepened.

My old patterns of thought were really the only problem I had. But I couldn't see that. I thought it was a "lack of business" problem. It was not. My thoughts were the problem. I began each day with a knot in my stomach.

My most scary thought each day originated in my childhood. It's a thought I see in others, and it's a thought that always undermines success. It's frightening, and it's based on a past truth. This is the thought: *The grown-ups have all the money!*

I'm a child again, emotionally. If I want anything at all I have to ask mom or dad. To get some baseball cards, money or candy, I have to be on their good side. Sometimes, if they are in bad moods, even if I've tried to please them and done my chores, no money. Not yet.

So a belief system sets in: the grown-ups have all the money in life. And to have any yourself, you have to get on their good side. This even runs deeper. It applies to food and shelter and whose house I'm going to stay at Saturday night. In order to have anything in life I have to please *them*. Life becomes a solitary mission: pleasing the grown-ups.

Fears begin in repeated thoughts like that and then they go underground. As an adult I technically knew that I myself was a grown-up, but it didn't ever feel like it. First of all I didn't have any money. And grown-ups, by definition, have the money.

So now I was older and always thinking if I don't have money myself it must mean that *I'm not a grown-up*. But wait. Was I not in my 30s and now 40s? How could a middle aged man not really be a grown-up? Deeper fears set in. Maybe there's something *wrong* with me. Really wrong, like a dark, hideous psychological disorder.

I went to a psychologist. I read books about the psychology of money. I went to a different psychologist. I learned energy tapping. I joined support groups on how to apply the principles of alcohol recovery to debts. I studied deeper. I took deep breathing classes. I hired coaches who specialized in money and debt. And still the fear remained. I'm incapable. I'm still a child.

Finally someone is staring me right in the eyes. He is shaking me by the shoulders. Wake up! Wake up! He is challenging me to snap out of it. He has asked me to create a bold assignment for myself. He asks me to create a new persona, a fearless provider of enormous service to others. He asks me to make a commitment . . . to make one and keep it no matter what. As if my life depended on it.

I didn't know you could live that way. That way I had so admired all my life in heroes. I didn't know that just anyone could do that. Certainly not me. With my history? How could I? Become the parent now in my relationship with myself? Grow myself up? Declare who I want to be? Then *be* that thing? Now? Eliminate the future? Be that fearless thing right now?

Chapter 15

Is this a game or is it real?

I received a rather shocking notice from the IRS about a large amount of money I owed now due in full. What? I thought I had a few more years to work it down!

I immediately went for a long walk with the enormous number in my head. Fear dominated my thoughts, but with every step I took the fear grew smaller. All my dire thoughts and beliefs about the number were challenged and turned away. Just thoughts.

I then became Robin Williams wanting to use that frightening six figure number as a towel. So I did. I created something beautiful around that number—an exciting project—and I came back from the walk with a fresh new feeling. If the project succeeded it would pay that whole bill.

My accountant was anxious.

"Don't you want to mortgage your house to pay this?" he urged. "Don't you want to do something more drastic?"

No, I'll just pay it all.

"Shouldn't I rather set up a long payment plan and go to the mat with them to avoid action on their part?"

No, I will just send them all the money.

So after a bit of action, the project worked. It was lovingly created and it gave such profound benefit to the people who received it that everybody won. Creating versus reacting!

What a useful concept! The ultimate life choice. Now I will keep that choice with me always. And I'll always remember one thing: reacting never builds anything for me. No stairway to heaven, no solution to anything. When I'm merely reacting to something I'm just reacting. Like a rat in a cage. Despite all my rage. When a problem arises I want to take it out for a walk, and watch the thoughts disappear and the solution emerge. Once I'm in action, doing any kind of movement, thoughts lift and fade like the fog and what is left is fearless.

Chapter 16

Be proud of your days as a junkie

A man we'll say is named Duke raised his hand in a seminar and said, "I've been a self-help junkie most of my life—Napoleon Hill, Tony Robbins, Wayne Dyer, the works. My friends and family mocked me. When is it going to be enough? I am doing well in my life now, but I wonder if they have a point."

I'd gotten to know Duke quite well prior to this seminar, and I could identify with him. Ever since a friend of mine showed me Napoleon Hill's *Master Key to Riches* in 1984, I myself have been hooked.

But why do I say hooked? And why did Duke use the word junkie? And why are motivational speakers and self-help authors sometimes distastefully mocked by the media, Hollywood and the arts?

Why does anyone do anything distasteful? Fear. Fear is at the bottom of all dysfunctional, unfriendly behavior. If you were not afraid you would not behave that way. If you didn't feel threatened, you'd be relaxed and kind. But only always.

Fear of self-help is like the fear felt by the out-of-shape-person, threatened by the condition of his own body. The out-of-shape person asking his in-shape friend, "Why do you have to work out so much?"

We only fear what we don't understand.

If you, too, are a "self-help" junkie, I do understand you. And please do not think poorly of yourself. You are an unusually brave and self-responsible person. Should you be mocked for constantly exploring your own potential? Is that really a negative thing? Or just something another person doesn't understand.

Most devoted readers of personal growth material are far better off because of it. Ask yourself what your life would be like today if you had *not* delved into self-exploration and self-improvement.

How would your body be today if you had never, ever exercised? It's the same question.

Because your mind benefits from exercise and stretching just as your body does. How many people do it with their minds, though? Not many. It's a powerful, creative thing to do, but not many do it. Most people don't realize how powerful it is. They went to school, and they think that should be enough.

What did they really learn at school about their minds? At best, they learned to deploy their brains as recording devices, playing back information at exam time.

But the best personal growth books and audio programs ask more than that. They ask you to consider changing everything! They ask that you attempt rigorous self-honesty and learn to grow. Personally. On your own time. In the face of your deepest fears. For no reason other than it will grow you. Not to please or manipulate anyone else.

It's not easy.

But this I know is true: self-help saved my life.

I mean that literally and truly. I was just self-destructively *lost* before I found it. I found Napoleon Hill, Earl Nightingale and Norman Vincent Peale . . . all those old guys who said you could take back your mind and rise above conditioning and create a positive, fearless career in the face of negative mobs of people who are begging you to join them as victims of circumstance. The Fraternal Order of the Disappointed.

I had just gotten sober, and I thought, what now? Yes it's wonderful to be clean and sober, but what about all these debts and no good employment history and no visible skills? And who am I to turn to? I had no idea how to be a self-responsible, successful . . . much less prosperous . . . adult.

And then self-help appeared. To save the day. To save my life.

Duke (my seminar attendee) said that prior to first reading *The Road Less Traveled* his own life was about pleasing his boss for eight hours then fearing he wouldn't please his family when he got home, an endless cycle of nervous anticipation. Always wondering what would win their approval. Anticipating their moods. Putting his head on their laps like a golden retriever would, looking up with sad doggy eyes to see if everything was okay. There, there, Duke, good dog. Good boy.

But sometimes, of course, it would be, "Bad dog!" and Duke's heart would race and he would jump back, and his spine would curve in anticipation of a good swat. That swat didn't hurt so much physically as it was just heartbreaking. All that trying-to-please out the window with one good verbal swat. That's the fate of those whose mission is to impress others.

The seeker in you seeks higher ground than that.

Chapter 17

Books have always changed lives

Pessimists mock books. They love saying, *you're not going to find it in books!* You need to get out there and live! Kick some butts! Pull your weight! Get your nose out of that ridiculous book and get real in the real world.

This is why pessimists remain pessimistic. They have no sense of learning or growth. Their book days ended right after school. What's for them to learn? Life is hard, so get over it. Get real. Move on. Life is a full-contact sport. No one gets out alive.

Those kinds of remarks used to shame me. That's the thing about fear. When you let it live in you, like a tumor in your gut, it causes you to feel shame very easily. Like every day. Whenever anyone says even the slightest thing that suggests you are not a man.

I was watching an interview with John Wooden on my TV screen late one night. It was one of the delightful add-on features of the DVD *We Are Marshall*. (I was watching the movie to learn more about courage. I succeeded.) I was touched by how many inspirational passages from books Wooden was quoting from memory. These were passages that helped shape him as the most successful basketball coach of all time. He didn't apologize for getting his inspiration from books. Nor did he call himself a self-help junkie.

In my life, crawling out of the cave of despair, one book led to another. Where would I find courage? How would I make a living? How could I succeed at anything after having been such a failure at everything? Do I try to remember what my two alcoholic parents taught me?

Books were the answer. Books taught me everything. You're not going to find it in books? Maybe you aren't, but I did.

Duke raises his hand again later in the day in the seminar by the lake. He wants to know how to eliminate his fear of financial insecurity and stop worrying so much about whether his little consulting business will "make it."

Picture yourself last week, Duke. You are sitting at your desk paralyzed with fear. It feels so bad you stand up and take a few breaths so you can upgrade the deep panic into a shallower, more manageable format: worrying. You drive to the post office to mail some bills and brochures, worrying the whole way there and back. You make yourself some coffee, worried as you stir in the cream. Now it's 43 straight minutes of worry.

Look back at those 43 minutes, Duke. Who was served? You have a real ability to help people—and when you do, wealth flows in to you—so what were these 43 minutes used for? Worrying! They were misused. Worry is a misuse of your imagination. You were focused on your own insecurities. Focused. On all the wrong things.

Focus is water from the hose, Duke. When you focus on your worries it grows more worry. Focus = H_2O! Why not focus on your clients? You'd grow more clients! Focusing on what you *want* to grow is the best use of your infinite mind. And if focus is water, then service is *sunshine* on your garden. So serve, don't worry. Just be useful. If you forget it you can create a song around it: Don't worry, be useful.

Duke is taking notes, writing like crazy as I speak. But Duke wonders. How will I keep this insight alive in my life? Then Duke starts to panic. I hand him a book. He thanks me. Read this book, I say. Whenever you feel scared that life is not going to work for you, I said, read something from this book.

Chapter 18

Harry was 93 and grief-stricken

Harry Bernstein was 93 years old and now very sad. His wife Ruby had just died of leukemia and . . . try as he might . . . he really couldn't come up with much of a will to live. What was the real point? To show the world how much sorrow an old man can bear from day to day? Even in this age of extended life, Harry thought 93 was very old. He had been with Ruby for 70 years.

How do you react when the person you have lived with and loved is suddenly gone? That's an interesting, frightening question, isn't it? Because it assumes you will do nothing but suffer. She is gone and life is so empty.

But Harry Bernstein did something unusual. Who knows what inspired him, but he decided to do something illogical. Oh, yes, he grieved; but not in a debilitating way.

He grieved, let us say, fearlessly.

In the face of such tragic sorrow, he was moved to pick up a pen and write. And all of a sudden something inside him took off. The way a kite rises against the wind. The way a person prays for and then is granted the courage to change the things he can.

Once Harry Bernstein decided to write he wrote and he wrote. Soon he couldn't wait to get up each day to write some more. What was this? What was happening?

He finally finished his manuscript he called "The Invisible Wall." It was the story of his life growing up in England and facing anti-Semitism, alcoholism in his family and all the adventures that carried him and Ruby to their final home in New Jersey. He mailed it to a publisher in New York and expected nothing.

New York publishers didn't give it a response at all (I know that feeling) so he sent it to the London office of Random House where it sat for over a year before it came across the desk of editor Kate Elton who said his book was "unputdownable."

The writing was fantastic. That's what "unputdownable" meant. The book was immediately published. At the age of 96 Harry Bernstein had begun life as a promising new author. Someone who the world found could really write.

Harry intuitively came out of the other side of grief and began creating. Building something that wasn't there before! What is greater courage than that? To walk into an empty space and build something that wasn't even *there* before?!? Day and night. Fearlessly. Against the wind. Rather than drowning in pity day and night. You might say Harry Bernstein did that for himself. But he also did it for you and me. How strange. By sitting alone in his empty, silent New Jersey home he did something for you and me.

Most people who try to "do something for" you and me would never think to do it alone in a silent New Jersey house. They would be in our face. Tracking you and me down and trying to impress us.

But Harry Bernstein instead merely inspired us. Funny how deeply you can reach others by bravely going inside rather than outside. Go deep enough and the whole world will roll at your feet.

Fatigue makes cowards
of us all.

Vince Lombardi

Chapter 19

A near fatal overdose of ecstasy

Whatever you think of former Massachusetts Governor Mitt Romney's politics, suspend that opinion for just a short moment. Set it aside and listen with a fresh ear. Because this event will take your breath away, no matter how you vote.

In July of 1996 Mitt Romney was a business leader going to work at his company called Bain Capital. One day, a day like any other day, the normal hustle and bustle of work was interrupted by a terrible shock. Romney's partner, Robert Gay, had found out that his 14-year old daughter was missing. It seems she had attended a rave party in New York City and had taken some ecstasy and now hadn't been seen or heard from in three days!

Most people who knew Robert Gay would be sympathetic. They would feel sorry for Robert. They'd tell him to take whatever time he needed to find his daughter. They might even give him a hug and say, "Keep me posted. Stay in touch. Anything I can do, you let me know."

Wouldn't we all do that? We'd think of how it would feel if our own daughter disappeared and we'd be startled at how empathetic we were. We'd even be a little prideful about how good we were to Robert in these terrifying times for him. We'd tell him we wanted to stay in touch. When we went home at night we'd sit with our family members and talk about how awful this must be for Robert and his wife. We'd shake our heads, take a deep breath, and after a while turn on *American Idol*. Sympathetic people trying to get a little rest before bed.

But that's not what Romney himself did. Upon hearing of Robert's missing daughter he jumped into action. He closed down his whole company and had all 30 partners and employees fly to New York to help find Robert Gay's daughter. He set up a command center in a hotel, hired a private detective firm to help their search, established toll-free numbers for tips and set up constant communication with the NYPD.

His employees also mobilized others in New York. They covered the city. Romney and his partners combed through Central Park, went door to door, talked to prostitutes, drug addicts, gang members, anyone who might have seen her.

Soon the posse of employees searching for the lost girl made the evening news. TV stations in New York showed photos of the missing girl and played video clips of Romney's employees fearlessly combing through the darkest regions of Central Park at night.

Then a break came in the case. A teenage boy called police headquarters to ask if there was a reward but then quickly hung up. The police traced the call to a home in Montville Township, New Jersey. Finally, some good news. They found Robert Gay's daughter, still alive, in the basement of that home. She was shivering through detox from massive doses of ecstasy. Doctors said she might not have lived another day.

Contrast this. Contrast this incident with how most business owners feel. Most business owners feel that even one half day of being shut down would be dangerous. Scary. A whole *day* shut down? Don't even consider it. Terrifying. What it might do to the month's cash flow. Can't afford it. We can't afford the bold move, the fearless act. There's too much at stake.

A lot of people wait a whole lifetime to prove themselves. They wait all their lives to be given a defining moment. To have the house across the street burn down so they can run out and save the little child from the fire. They wait. And wait. They know they'd shine if they were given a chance. Or at least they hold out some hope for that.

They don't see. Houses are burning every day. There isn't a day that goes by where there isn't an opportunity. In large ways and very small. To be fearless.

Chapter 20

Dance me through the panic

I suffered from something a few years ago that I can only describe as a fear. It was a fear of communicating with others for the express purpose of having money leave their pockets and come into mine.

Let's call it a fear of selling. Oh, I was not alone. I noticed it in others, too. My clients, associates, friends, and respected contemporaries all seemed to have it too! So what was the problem?

In a simple, single short word the problem was this: need.

Need!

Need was the problem because that acute *sense of need* was what was leading to the *fear*.

When you think you *need* something you will get scared. To need is to be scared. That's it; in a formulaic nutshell: Need = scared. (Am I memorizing these formulae? I can use all of them in my journey: focus = water, service = sunshine, need = scared.)

So the answer to this fear was to not *need* money. To not need to make the sale. Simple and clean. I don't need it. I can now just get into action creating it. Creating! Everyone loves creating things. Deep down it's fun and satisfying. I remember the first thing I ever made in wood shop class

. . . some awkward flower holder thing . . . I kept it for decades. Creation charms the soul.

So first I would "create a new distinction" around selling so it was no longer selling to me. I wasn't afraid of creating, I was just afraid of selling. Or rather, some idea I had called selling. Repeat: (for me, so I don't forget) I was afraid of *the idea of* selling.

That's the thing about the things we fear. It's always the idea of them. Therefore they are always experienced worse in our heads than out there in the world. Funny, but the real world is kinder and more supportive than the mind itself is. There is no real fear out there in the world, it turns out. It is all in the mind. If that isn't humorous I don't know what is.

The real world welcomed Harry Bernstein's writing with open arms. The real world loved him and didn't care that he was 93 or 96 or whatever number the mind latches onto to scare itself with. Something out there in the real world is always ultimately going to be supportive. But let that same thing fester in the *mind*? It will bring fear.

We think we need money; not realizing we'd be all right without it. (Once you know you are all right without something you will increase its flow into your life. It's thinking you need it that stops it.)

We think we need love, too. We think love is necessary for life. Same as money. So I saw Sally across the crowded floor at the school dance but I didn't ask her to dance because something necessary-to-life might have gotten rejected. I couldn't bear to lose what I thought I needed. It's all in the mind, though. Love and money. Because we think we need it we fear losing it before we even have it and therefore *we don't create.*

The Dalai Lama takes creative action. He travels the world bravely communicating to whomever will listen about his beloved spirituality and lost homeland of Tibet—a homeland that was ruthlessly invaded and taken over by Chinese communists.

People ask the Dalai Lama why he doesn't feel angrier. *They took over your country—why can't you be angry with them? They took your country!*

"Why should I give them my mind as well?" he said.

So I decided to keep creative possession of my own mind as well. I took the most fun thing I was then doing in my professional life—my most fun and favorite thing—the question and answer sessions during a seminar, and I just did a series of those with sales prospects and substituted that activity for selling. I'd get a prospect on the phone and I'd ask questions and answer questions like I was in a seminar and it was a lot of fun and a lot of coaching and training deals got signed very quickly. It felt like I was dancing.

When someone would object to my offer of a proposal, I would double-down. I'd agree with the objection! I'd dance with them wherever they wanted to go on the floor! And if someone said my price was a problem, I'd agree with them and immediately *raise* it! I'd say I was undervaluing the work and would never do that again. Highly unorthodox. I'd developed a habit of creating. As an antidote to fear. Objection? Agree. Price not right? Raise it! (Byron Katie once said that if you are wrongfully arrested for murder, you can just tell the cops, "Right person, wrong incident.")

Fearlessness has you dancing *with* the situation instead of fighting against it. No matter what it is. Even the great martial artists know not to directly resist an opponent's force, but rather to dance with the force. Let the force from the outside join the fearless force on the inside. Have everything dance with the heart you have inside.

Dance me to your beauty
with a burning violin

Dance me through the panic
till I'm gathered safely in

Lift me like an olive branch
and be my homeward dove

Dance me to the end of love

Leonard Cohen

Chapter 21

We really don't need Robin Hood

Ayn Rand was brutal. A very courageous woman who wrote powerful novels like *The Fountainhead* and *Atlas Shrugged* that were filled with her bold philosophies of freedom, self-responsibility and the capacity each of us has to create success in life. But brutal.

She hated the legend of Robin Hood. She hated it that Robin Hood "assumed a halo of virtue by practicing charity with wealth he did not own."

I hear politicians running for office today assuming the same halo that Ms. Rand despised in Robin Hood. They act saddened by the plight of the average citizen who works for a living. They promise to bring an end to that. It's an unconscionable situation, whatever it may be. Just give the politician the power, and (s)he will do the rest. Vote correctly, and you're home free. Life will have nothing to do with you anymore.

Ayn Rand said that Robin Hood "became a justification for every mediocrity who, unable to make his own living, had demanded the power to dispose of the property of his betters, by proclaiming his willingness to devote his life to his inferiors at the price of robbing his superiors."

Ouch. How do I feel when I think of myself as a mediocrity? Let me check my feelings out. Oh yeah ouch. I reflect about it deeper, and realize that there was never a comic book hero in my youth called Mediocre Man with a big grey M on his jersey.

When I'm doing too much thinking about myself, I'm not in action. Nor am I creating the courage to change the things I can. Soon I'm thinking of myself as a mediocrity (mainly because I am one), and it gets even worse because now I can't even see myself as *capable* of good, true action.

But anyone . . . even I . . . can take action. I don't need Robin Hood to take something from someone else and give it to me. And how do I get myself to take action? By taking it. Doing it! Doing it causes the doing of it.

Chapter 22

Before birth and after death

The prolific, brilliant author Anthony Burgess believed that we had plenty of time to be lazy before we were born—and that there will be even more time for that after we die. "Wedged as we are," he said, "between two eternities of idleness, there is no excuse for being idle now."

Writers are often idle. Even professional novelists suffer from something they call "writer's block." (Their excuse for being idle now.) They feel blocked because they don't realize that they have to drop their egos to write well. That's why it's often so hard for them. (Many writers have been clients of mine and we work on why it's hard for them to be writers). The ego doesn't want you creating a new world, especially creating new *people*! Because the ego holds the copyright for that. The made-up human being. It feels violated and infringed upon by extremely creative acts. That's why it takes such courage to create. Even to sit down and write a song. Bring in music where there was no music. What could be a more fearless act?

Try it. Try creating a made-up story and see how it first gets resisted. I can't *do this* I used to cry out in the face of creating something. Write a song. Anything. A new career, a new book, a new agreement with my daughter . . . anything creative. I can't do this. I am . . . *blocked*!

So, being blocked, therefore, idle isn't just for novelists. The opportunity to fester in the condition known as blocked is here and now for us all. But so is the way out. So is the courage to create. You can create anytime, anywhere. Just start bringing beauty into existence that wasn't there before. Any profession, any task, you can do it. Start creating a *new you* unrelated to your personality, then add in new worlds and alternative universes and watch how you make the ego very nervous—the ego wants you to stick to the preexisting story.

I once wrote a book about the story of you because I wanted you (and me) to see that no matter how honest you are the story of you will always be a few steps behind reality and therefore false. Which is why Jesus didn't need or want to write a book about himself. You won't find a book called "The Story of Me" by Jesus . . . nor did he have to pass out brochures after raising Lazarus from the dead. He never promoted himself saying, "There's even *more* I can do!" Instead his message was the opposite. There's more **you** can do. Even more than he was doing.

He didn't need to promote himself because when one's actions are that stunningly poetic people won't forget. He was not idle. When you are not idle, the world will find out about *you*, too, without a lot of promotion on your part. They're still talking about Lazarus two thousand years later. Do your equivalent. Raise somebody up.

Chapter 23

Why would you turn to cannibalism?

After reading some very inspiring books about the benefits of fasting, I started trying it out. I went on a 20-day juice fast monitored by an internet site that sent tons of emails to me every week to redirect my mind when it thought it needed solid food.

Why fast? Well, for one thing researchers at Yale Medical School have discovered that hungry mice take in information more quickly than well-fed mice. Fasting mice retain that information better as well. I read that report thinking back on my childhood hero Mighty Mouse. We never saw him eating. Did we?

The Yale researchers pointed out that our thinking abilities deteriorate after a big meal. No great surprise here. Blood cells rush from the brain area like rats from a sinking ship when the stomach is filled with food. The act of digestion does more to cloud the mind than any bong.

The great whirling dervish poet Rumi recommended fasting, too. He said, "If the brain and belly are burning clean with fasting, every moment a new song comes out of the fire. The fog clears, and new energy makes you run up the stairs in front of you."

So for a year I have studied various aspects of fasting and fasted in various ways. Wonderful experiences! And like every other challenge in life, fear is the only problem with it.

People can actually go for 30 days without food and be just fine. So it's all in the mind. *Fear* of not eating is the real problem. We read about a small plane crashing in the mountains and after seven days, there's cannibalism! People start tearing bodies apart and eating each other! When all they need is water. Just eat that snow, darn it! That's all you need! But because of the *thoughts* in their heads they are tearing their fellow human beings from limb to limb and eating them. Because of the thoughts in their heads.

Amazing what thoughts can do. They are the only things worth fearing.

I've got more energy now
than when I was younger because
I know exactly what I want to do.

George Balanchine

Chapter 24

This insane posse of clowns

There's a spooky imaginary source for much of my fear. It's a fake construct that pretends it's true. It's an unreal thing. And because it's not even real, it is impossible to protect it from harm. It is what I call my personality.

I'm frightened and defensive because of it. It feels like a costume I'm sewn into. What was once hastily formed in my childhood mind to give me a sense of safe identity and separation now, in later life, becomes a trap. Like being imprisoned inside a puppet; or stitched into a clown suit.

When I work with people who want to succeed but are not succeeding, one of the things I can see getting in the way is the character they believe themselves to be. Usually it's a personality they formed in the early years. But they think it's very current. It's what they believe they *are* and have to always be.

Where did they *get* this thing?

It started with what they were told about themselves! Maybe they were told early on that they were lazy, or good, or bad, or that they were disorganized, or that they were cowardly, or that they weren't very thoughtful. These opinions were then assimilated as personality traits! Other people's judgments! How could *that* be who a person really is?

There's no reality to those critical, negative judgments because people only make them when they're in a bad mood. Isn't that true? When you are in a good mood, feeling wonderful, you have no desire to go around judging anyone. You're having too much fun to do that. It's got to happen when you are in a bad mood. That's always when judgment happens.

Therefore, personalities are formed by other people's bad moods.

But that's actually okay, because personalities aren't real anyway. In fact, in a crunch all these "characteristics" that you think make you who you are . . . are dropped! In a real bind, you just move to action. You damn the torpedoes of personality. You're full speed ahead! Your old story of who you are is just sitting there like a pile of discarded clothing . . . like Clark Kent's business suit crumpled in a pile on the floor of a phone booth.

Once again, look at the house burning down across the street. See how you run out of my house and hear a small child crying over in that other house inside the flames and you run in, grab the child and crawl back out. It all happens so fast. There wasn't much time to think. You did it all in a state of action.

What was your personality doing at that time? Was it even around? What? It disappeared? You were simply swept up in the fierce thrill of what you felt ought to be done.

Yes that's what being fearless is. It's a dropping of personality. It replaces it with the fierce thrill of doing what ought to be done. Fearless isn't a personal quality. It's not a trait inside any single person. It's as much there for you as it is for that brave person you've always admired.

I remember being in a crowded shopping mall with my children a few years ago and we were near a very long and tall escalator in a department store and we heard screaming and I saw a small boy sitting on the escalator his pants caught in the metal at the top of the moving stair, and I ran up the stairs and pulled him free, knowing I was tearing his pants and flesh but just doing it while his parents and other shoppers just stood by frozen with horror at his screams and predicament. I carried him down to where an employee directed me to an emergency clinic area in the mall and a nurse cleaned and patched up his bleeding little butt and said he would be okay. His parents couldn't stop thanking me, and my kids were saying, "Wow, dad, you rocked."

And when I thought back to it, after I came to my senses and re-settled into the everyday personality, I realized that I had acted without being anyone. If I had been *me* I might not have gone after that boy.

Chapter 25

You misunderstand your own excitement

I remember now that my coach Steve Hardison would sometimes break the paradigm of personality by asking me not to be me.

When I tried to explain why I wasn't doing something that had to be done I would say, "Well, I'm not good at it" or I'd say, "I'm scared about it" and he would sit back and think. Then he would say, "Well, then don't be you." I would look puzzled, and he would continue, "Be someone else; someone other than you. Someone else entirely who is doing it. Be Brando or be DeNiro or be someone who *could* do it."

Now, this sounded really bizarre. Like I'm going to be a total phony?

Then I thought to myself, *Well, you are anyway* . . . so you might as well be a phony who can get something done. Being the person who *can't* do it is being even phonier because you're pretending you're incapable. Why not make up someone who would serve you instead of feeling like you're stuck in someone who does not?

Fear can be outwitted. Fear is not final. My friend Rebecca just wrote this to me, "Fritz Perls once said that fear is misunderstood excitement. When we contemplate change, we get a bubble of energy. If we are in a state of well-being, we will feel exhilarated by that energy. If we are insecure, we will get frightened."

I loved that. Fear is misunderstood excitement. Maybe I'm not afraid after all; maybe I'm just excited. I'm excited at the idea of doing something I've never done . . . of being Brando in *One Eyed Jacks* and just being fearless.

Because my own personality is just a mirage formed by repeated thoughts. And in the moment called *now* I can drop all of that, and I can be *whoever I need to be* given the higher purpose, the greater goal, and what I am up to, and the exciting game I am in.

Utopia is on the horizon; I walk two steps, it takes two steps back. I walk ten steps, and it is ten steps further away. What is utopia for? It is for this, for walking.

Eduardo Galeano

Chapter 26

You taught me not to be afraid

We just learned about an actor who was suffering pancreatic cancer and only has five months to live. He's lucky, I thought. No one is guaranteed tomorrow, and yet he's been given five months! Has anyone given *me* five months to live? Ever? I think not.

What would we do with a guaranteed five months? That's almost too much life to think about. We worry about longevity and hope for eternity while not knowing what to do with ourselves in the next hour.

I like reading. It's something I can do with myself in the next hour that will have me emerge strengthened and emboldened. So I turn to my file of good clippings. I save what encourages me. Here's a clipping from a recent *USA Today* article. The interviewer asked Ronald Reagan's daughter Patti Davis if her father ever got rattled. She said, "No. He wasn't scared of anything, even as he suffered from Alzheimer's disease. I went to visit him and talked to him about the days that he'd take me to the ocean as a little girl and teach me to body surf. These were really huge enormous waves. I told him, 'You taught me not to be afraid.' He laughed and said, 'There's nothing to be afraid of!' I think that sums up his approach to life, even as he approached death."

That's it! Fearless isn't a quality . . . it's an approach.

The fruit of the spirit is love, joy and peace. To be stripped, poor, to have nothing, to be empty—this transforms nature; the void causes water to climb mountains and performs many other marvels of which we would not now speak.

Meister Eckhart

Chapter 27

You may call me a dreamer

I was watching Oprah on TV and she was saying that she left her church the minute she heard her preacher say that his God was a *jealous god*. She saw jealousy as a human thing, not something God would stoop to. She saw jealousy as a less than divine state. A dysfunctional indulgence by fearful people here on earth. If the God of that church was like that, then she was going to have to bounce.

She had a mind that was free enough to do that.

The canvas of a free mind is often empty. It is what Meister Eckhart described as being stripped and poor. The empty canvas is void of paint, markings, thought. (And yes that's you, in your wildest dreams, and in reality.)

The mind is a canvas upon which you can now paint your precise and ideal scene. Don't procrastinate on this painting because of fear. Without you becoming an artist, your mind can't serve you. The mind does not solve general problems or achieve vague or general goals. You can paint a life scene full of color and precision, like a Chinese painting, an act of such courage it will startle you.

The void—that mind of yours—causes water to climb mountains.

It's possible to live as fearlessly as Neale Donald Walsch once said, "Nothing is going to spoil this moment . . . imagine making that decision: nothing's going to spoil this moment. Now, imagine making that decision about a relationship, job, day in the week, or . . . whatever. Imagine applying that idea uniformly in your life."

He could say it even more simply: Imagine living fearlessly.

Chapter 28

Conformity is a waste of time

The truth we find in fiction can be exhilarating and inspiring, like the fictional character of Jack Reacher in the wonderful adventure mysteries of Lee Child. Kathy and I have gone to see Mr. Child speak twice at the Poisoned Pen Bookstore in Scottsdale and he is so bright and inspiring. I love hearing how he writes his books . . . where does the courage to create come from?

He says his brave, uncompromising hero, Jack Reacher, is who he himself would like to be. To build the character, he takes himself and multiplies the courage factor by ten. The result? Jack Reacher. In fact, in a crisis, when I'm trying to decide between courage and being a chicken I often ask myself, "What would Reacher do?"

I always thought it would be fun to write mystery novels. And then I went into fear. What if nobody reads them? What if all the time I spent on them was wasted? What if I looked stupid?

But if I'm to be fearless I'll just write them. It's only the *thought* that has me be afraid. It's funny that everyone I've ever known who is a writer starts out by being afraid to write something. But when they are writing it they are not afraid. It's only thinking about it that makes them afraid. Doing it does not. It's the same with me. While writing, I am no longer afraid.

Even as I wrote the part about the actor with five months to live being lucky compared to you and me who are not even guaranteed tomorrow, I thought I might seem heartless and insensitive to say that. I then thought, if I'm too afraid to finally put that in this book, *I'll give the thought over to one of my fictional characters in my other book.* That's how so much truth gets into fiction.

A book is called fearless and the author is afraid to put something in it?

The author betrays himself as a coward, but continues to write?

Seems to be happening.

Chapter 29

Exactly how is it that art saves lives?

Art saves lives. The courage to create means everything.

Ballet is an art. And the great ballet master George Balanchine said something I'll never forget. As he entered his later years he said he had more energy now than when he was younger because he now knows exactly what he wants to do.

I would only want to read that quote ten times a day. So much wisdom in it and so many secrets revealed to living life as a masterpiece.

Balanchine's quote reminded me of watching the mesmerizing Ken Burns documentary on the life of architect Frank Lloyd Wright. It was fascinating to see his life and art and creative energy take off while he himself was in his 80s, after the world of architecture had written him off as a has-been. Such beautiful designs pouring out of him in his later years, as his art was making him younger and younger as years flew by. "I can't turn them out fast enough" he said of the many buildings he designed into his 90s.

The Bob Dylan line I now recall is "I was so much older then . . . I'm younger than that now." Maybe all Frank Lloyd Wright's new energy came from knowing exactly what *he* wanted to do. It wears you out to do what others want you to do. It totally fatigues you to try to anticipate what would please and pacify people all around you. That wears the body down. Being bold and focused is what creates energy. The fearless decision to do exactly what *you* want to do.

Whosoever is delighted in solitude
is either a wild beast or a god.

Francis Bacon

Chapter 30

And then my heart stood still

I feel like I'm in a scene from *The English Patient* as our small plane flies between mountains into the tiny patch of landing strip in Ketchum, Idaho. Am I scared? Well, yeah!

So is it true that all fear like this emerges from thought? Isn't some fear something you just feel? Like the minute I see the mountains?

Maybe it *is* just a thought: I think I might crash. Get hurt or die. Embarrass myself by yelling while the other passengers stoically pray. It's not an elaborate thought. Not carefully considered. In fact it's so quick a thought that I don't know I thought it. It seems like I looked out the window at the mountains we were between and I just felt it.

This is the big confusion.

In all of life.

Where fear comes from.

Because we think it's from the plane and the mountains. It sure feels that way. So we keep a lookout! We survey the people and the places outside our windows to assess the next threat to our security—emotional or physical, it doesn't matter. And by doing this all our lives, we miss the role of thought.

We think the fear is from the plane and the mountains so we take a car trip next time. Rearranging the outside circumstances to make the inside feel better. Now we're experiencing many, many long hours of driving. That's a version of rearranging the deck chairs. Change the external and maybe the internal (the fear inside) will leave.

And how is that working for me right now? Oh, but it isn't.

Because while I'm driving I am now listening to the audiobook version of *Feel the Fear and Do It Anyway*. A woman named Susan Jeffers is asserting that fear will never go away. That as long as you live, you will experience fear. She says, "Every time you take a step into the unknown you experience fear."

Holy cow. Is that true? Jeffers says it is. But is it? She says that "fear is part of the package" and you better get used to it. But whose package is she referring to? Everyone's? Mine?

I know that many children try new, unknown things with no experience of fear whatsoever. I used to watch my children do it. I'll never forget little Jessica, who couldn't swim at the time, just fearlessly jumping into the deep end of a public pool before I could stop her. I stood in amazement as she swam happily to the edge. I know adults who do the same. Some older people fearlessly embark on new, unknown ventures while others run in the other direction.

But Susan Jeffers thinks that shouldn't be happening. Her position is that you are simply always going to be afraid. It's part of this scary human package. So let's learn to deal with it. Let's drive ourselves hard enough to overcome fear, push through it and tough it out. Her final philosophy is that "pushing through fear is less frightening than living with the bigger underlying fear that comes from a feeling of helplessness!"

So Susan Jeffers says these are my frightening choices in life—1) Doing terrifying things that scare me to do them or 2) Living with the even bigger underlying fear that comes from feeling helpless.

That's quite a choice. Which life would you rather live? It reminds me of Woody Allen's comical statement that "Life is divided up into the horrible and the miserable." But that was supposed to be a joke.

For years and years I would have been among the millions who have bought Susan's book and her story that fear is a given. *It's always there.* Get used to it. In my earlier years of working with my clients I used to assume that "truth"—fear is part of the package! —and our options are to overcome the fears or suffer the everlasting helpless feeling of being a coward.

So I began to learn to push through fears and tough things out. To overcome. I shall *overcome*! First this fear, then that one. And I tried to help fearful clients do the same. And then new fears would rise up and once again the choice of life would be between the horrible and the miserable.

When I began integrating the writings of Ken Wilber and the work of Byron Katie into my own life and the lives of my clients I began to see some new choices. I began to see that fear was *not* necessary. It did not have to be "part of the package." I learned the role of thought. So rather than feeling the fear and doing it anyway—how about feeling the fear and looking for the thought that causes it?

There is something better than heaven. It is the eternal, meaningless, infinitely creative mind. It can't stop for time or space or even joy. It is so brilliant that it will shake what's left of you to the depths of all-consuming wonder.

Byron Katie

Chapter 31

Calling Byron Katie

I had never experienced a single human being who was fearless. Until I met Katie. Day after day in the school of hers that I attended, she was up there leading us morning through night, intelligent, sweet and calm, and without fear. Without worry. Just peaceful energy. I had never experienced anyone like her.

Months went by after that school and I saw her speak again at a gathering that Steve Hardison arranged for friends and family. She remembered me from the school. I got to know her husband the author Stephen Mitchell and the more I used her system called the work (www.thework.com) the more fear began to disappear in my life and in the lives of my clients.

Katie later invited me to call her at her home to discuss this book. She knew I was writing about the relationship between thought and fear, and she was delighted to help me with my key question: how can fear come from a thought when it feels deeper than that? It feels like sometimes I'm feeling it *before* I think anything. Like the moment I looked out the plane windows in Idaho and felt the plane dip and saw the mountains on either side of us. The bottom dropped out of my stomach before I could *form* a thought. Or so it felt.

People all call her Katie, but Byron Kathleen Reid is her real natural born Irish name. Some people see the name Byron and think it's a faux-medieval affectation. They are wrong. Some people hear about her and think she's a new age guru of some sort, but they are wrong there, too. She is as humble as anyone I've ever known. When she first answered the phone and I said, "Is this Katie?" she said, "That's what I am told." When a woman once asked her in a small gathering how she handles her fame as an author, she said in all sincerity, "That's just a rumor to me so I don't pay any attention."

I told her how much her school had relaxed and changed me. The experience had made everything fresh and new. The peaceful energy I now had! I was so much older when I went to her school. I'm younger than that now. I now knew exactly what I wanted to do. Live this moment. Write this book about fear.

We talked for a time about the mind's need to label and judge everything. At her school she taught us to take a morning walk with no mind. To label things anew as we saw them. As if we were empty children without stories. Then from the void: Tree. Sky. Lamppost. Woman. Love.

She reminded me that the mind is a polarity. On one end of the pole is the "I know" mind; the ego. But on the other end is the innocent, open, "I don't know" mind. Sometimes experienced as a loving heart.

The "I know" mind thinks it knows everything, especially a threat when it sees one. It tells me to be careful. Of this person and that. Of financial risk. It tells me I might lose everything! Or, I might not get published. I might waste my time. I could look foolish! That's the "I know" mind at work. Judging all day.

But the relaxed "I don't know" mind loves being a student. Of everyone. So I'm on this phone call with Katie because she knows something I don't. I told Katie that her "work"—a four-question process she teaches for undoing the worried thoughts and finding freedom—reminded me of Ramana Maharshi's advice that we all use inquiry to get to enlightenment. He recommended asking "Who am I?" over and over until we found out.

Katie agreed that that would work if you stayed with it but she said the western mind does not always have the patience to do so. However, her own simple process allows the ego to participate in its own undoing. Katie's work allows the ego to cross-examine itself. The ego loves being a famous attorney.

I immediately pictured my ego as a lawyer . . . I thought about the lawyers for O.J. Simpson. At first they were called the "Dream Team." They loved that phrase. Famous lawyers who lined up to show off their skills on national television during the trial of the century. It doesn't get much better than that for a lawyer. And they were indeed impressive. Arguing this small point and that. Challenging witnesses dramatically. Flairs and booming boastful rhetorical flourishes for the whole nation to admire and for the jury to be hypnotized by.

But they eventually participated in their own undoing. Just like the ego seduction of Katie's work. Because anyone watching could see O.J. was guilty of murder. (This was later confirmed in the civil trial by an overwhelming preponderance of evidence.)

So these "I know" lawyers had now set a murderer free. They thought we were impressed by them, but every time we looked at them we saw their own undoing. They couldn't do anything without the blood of the murder victims appearing on the backdrop of our imagination. In the end, the ego participates in its own undoing.

I said to Katie that her work—her four questions—made me think of these things. Made me think of a courtroom in which we trick an egotistical lawyer into arguing the opposite of his own case.

"Yes," she said. "Because in the end there is no case."

Then I asked Katie if her work could eliminate a certain visceral, phobic fear I had. She asked me gentle questions about it and led me through a subset of questions that would undo that fear (see her book *Loving What Is* for those questions that dive below the four questions). I told her I had always believed that some of my fears were beyond thought. That my deepest fears simply arise before there's time to think. From my cells, it felt like.

"But cells are just a thought," she said.

"But then from where?" I asked her. Because fear seems like it can hit us in the stomach faster than a human can possibly think. Like when flying between two mountains in Idaho.

"But you thought *before*," she said. "Before that feeling. Back in your history. Or else you couldn't be afraid now. Be with it and go back to your earliest thoughts," she said. "Do the work on *those* thoughts. Take your time."

And as we talked more I was overtaken by a strange peace. A grace. Amazing. I thought back to her nine-day school when after so many hours of work we relaxed by singing along with Arlo Guthrie's soul-stirring version of "Amazing Grace."

I had a final question for Katie on this call. What happens when the "I know" egoic mind dissolves? After the work and the thought that is causing the fear has been undone and shown to simply not be true. When wisdom arises and there is no more need to worry or judge?

"Then it's . . . humorous . . . " said Katie. "That's the only word I can think of at the moment. Humorous." I thought I could hear her laughing quietly.

Chapter 32

All the grim macho elephant hunting

I love this solitude right now, being alone as I am in Idaho. So I decide to walk the streets of Ketchum before the sun goes down. I see a big banner over the street that says "Ernest Hemingway Days Celebration!" I realize that Hemingway lived here in his last days on earth. Amazing how a writer's name and fame lives on if there's enough power in his work.

All the grimly self-promotional macho elephant-hunting, boxing shenanigans Hemingway displayed while drunk as a celebrity-writer were *nothing* compared to the power he put into his work alone at his typewriter. All that ego-promotion was folly compared to the fearless moment facing the blank page in the early morning. (He used to count his words written each day. Some people think that was pathetic, but I think it was brave.)

In the end it's not the ego's personal publicity campaign that finds power. It's not the extroverted showing off that achieves transcendence. It's the work. What happens when you are alone with the work.

As I walked alone I thought of Elvis Presley. Sam Phillips owned Sun Records in Memphis when the young, unknown Elvis Presley first came in to try to make a record. When Sam Phillips recalled those days he once said, "Now, you've got to keep in mind that Elvis Presley was probably, innately, the most introverted person that came into that studio. Because he didn't play with bands. He didn't go to this little club and pick and grin. All he did was sit with his guitar on the side of his bed at home."

I pictured a lonely Elvis at the edge of his bed, playing his guitar and singing, getting better and better and better. So many people waste their lives running around picking and grinning. I told myself: Stay home until it feels right. Sit with your guitar on the side of the bed. For hours, years if you need to. You'll know when you're ready to connect.

Such a huge key to success lies in Hemingway's solitary word-counting discipline. In working on the art. All by himself down at the end of his own lonely street in Idaho counting his words. Not in the promotion of the art. In the courageous solitude of the work.

Just the other night watching *The Croupier* the Clive Owen character quotes Hemingway at a crucial moment, "Sometimes, when a man is broken, he becomes stronger in the broken parts." And I realized that he was quoting from Hemingway's work . . . the writing itself . . . not the promotional legend.

So I walk the streets of Ketchum thinking all these things and getting closer to the Hemingway banner. They say that Hemingway loved the sports and woods of Ketchum. He appealed to many men in his day because his public persona and his celebrity story seemed so brazen. He was a boxer. A bullfight aficionado. A heavy rough and tumble drinker. Fearless, it seemed.

And then he blew his brains out with a shotgun. Afraid to live another day.

Too much self-promotion, and too little writing in his later years. His body is here. It occurs to me as I walk under the banner. At Trail Creek Campground, you can hear water rushing over rocks while you look at his gravesite. In the fall of 1939, Hemingway finished *For Whom the Bell Tolls* right here where I'm walking around. It was written in Suite 206 of the Sun Valley Lodge (the lodge where I would be doing my seminar.) Don't ask for whom the bell tolls; it tolls for thee.

And it tolls for me.

Because the message in Hemingway's life was a message for me to receive. The more I made a big promotional deal about myself, the more fearful I would become. Whenever I built up my story, I increased the fear of that house of cards tumbling down and leaving me with nothing. Because stories are made of nothing.

But when I simply put courage into the work itself . . . then it's different. Then a strange absence of fear settles in. I look up from the page in the solitary morning. I feel nothing but lightness. I seem to be floating above the world. The broken parts are stronger. This is fearless.

Chapter 33

Yes, but what will I get?

I am here in Idaho to do some consulting with the Sun Valley Summer Symphony and help them raise money. They don't really need me because they are already very successful—but they enjoy my consulting anyway, and I have to say that Sun Valley may be the most beautiful place on earth, with more rolling shapes and colors than the eye can take in.

The symphony (which offers summer concerts free to the public) has been incorporating a radical form of fundraising called relation-shift, first proposed in the book of the same name by Mike Bassoff and myself. It asks the fundraiser to focus more on the giving than the getting. In other words to play around with being fearless. Because those who focus more on giving than getting become daring creators.

It's hard for most people to believe it would work. (That's where being fearless comes in. You have to try something that has no guarantee of succeeding. You have to be willing to give with no thought of return. Like Hemingway alone in his room, giving his heart to his writing with no guarantee that the book will sell or be read by anyone.)

Most people focus on the big get. They want to *know* what their efforts will *get* them. But the final truth is surprising: life focused on what you're going to *get* is always less abundant than life focused on what you can *give*. Because the one (giving) requires creativity and courage, while the other (getting) is just another form of fear.

Chapter 34

No fear like money fear

Fear welled up in me as I was signing a book of mine that I was about to send to a poet. The poet was a friend, but still, he was a poet. And my book was about money. Wasn't it comparatively shallow of me to write a book about money?

Pretty embarrassing, as I thought more about it. To write a book about wealth when I could be doing something more poetic. But then I sobered my mind up a bit. I thought about Dylan Thomas' life. He was so obsessed with money . . . always being in debt and borrowing money and then getting drunk and never paying the money back. All those letters of his that I read where he is asking people for money, instead of writing poetry, instead of creating.

All the poets, artists, singers, writers, entrepreneurs, stay-at-home business moms, fundraisers, saints, helpers, seekers and good people who were heartbroken over money. And what lack of money made them do to their families and friends. Soon I knew I was on the right path. There is poetry in money, if it's approached without fear. That had taken me so many years to learn. And my book was passing it on. My fear of what the poet would think disappeared. I signed the book this way:

Money breaks the heart. Until it becomes an art.

Chapter 35

Laughing all the way to the bank

Often the first step to releasing fear is to see the humor and laugh. Which is why I almost always start discussions of money with this quote from Rita Rudner: "Someday I want to be rich. Some people get so rich they lose all respect for humanity. That's how rich I want to be."

Now let me go put on some music before I continue discussing this. I want to expand upon that concept of money as art. Where's the music I want? Oh here it is: You never give me your money; you only give me your funny paper. My *Abbey Road* album is cranked up now for me to continue.

You want to make this sale. You think you *need* this money. You are nervous, but you have all your selling points in mind. You have the exact dollar figure you will accept. You meet with the potential buyer. It seems to be going great. But he objects to your price! Then, in the middle of negotiation, you break down.

Why? Fear? Something started weighing so heavily on your heart. And lungs. Your breathing became labored. You had a hard time finishing sentences without gulping for fresh air. You felt a cold in your chest.

No one seems to realize that money doesn't have to be this way. That a lighter approach actually works better; that humor dissolves fear. That humor is as high as spirit itself on the level of consciousness—it's just that nobody can see it. People laugh nervously when you even mention humor and spirit in the same breath.

A Phil Keaggy song called *Portrait of a Christian* asks about how we know we are in the presence of the Holy Spirit. The song asks:

"Is it a beatific smile?"

"A holy light upon your brow?"

"Oh, no."

"I felt His presence when you laughed just now."

Chapter 36

Why am I living like a caged animal?

Fear drops me down into the worried mind where I spend my days fire-fighting; trying to extinguish life's little difficulties. This is not a powerful place to be. Putting out fires. But sometimes I do it. All the livelong day.

Soon I feel a blazing backdraft of fire: The bank calls . . . I'm overdrawn . . . the doctor calls . . . I'm overweight. Fires. Okay now they're out. The money's transferred. The fasting worked. Fires ahead?

Well, there *will be* if I don't get out of my worried mind. How do I get out? If you gave me your money would that do it? Would that satisfy my mind? One rich man in a hundred, the song says, has a satisfied mind. So no. This fire fighting comes from fear itself, not from real fires. They are mirages. Fire images on the water.

So fighting them is essentially negative activity. A double negative: trying to make the *bad* thing *go away*.

I'm going to shift to neutral. The fearless state. I'll get my DVD of *The Secret* out and watch it again. That will take me back to neutral. There's been a backlash against *The Secret* but I don't care because I love this movie and the way it always inspires me; it takes me up the ladder over fear. It is so exciting to watch a visually artistic movie on how the mind really works. It wakes me up to the power of imagination.

I know what the critics are saying. They're saying *The Secret* is not the answer to everything. (It's amazing how angry people get when something is not the answer to everything.) Of course it's not the answer to everything.

If you watch *The Secret* or listen to Esther Hicks channeling the law of attraction you might begin to believe that you can have anything you want just by imagining it. Picture something, and it's yours! Picture a Mercedes and game over . . . it's in your driveway. No, we're not kidding . . . go *look*!

Well. You begin to see the problem. *The Secret*, dramatic as it is, is only a first step. Step one is to get the picture. So necessary a step, and such a neglected step . . . but . . . it's not the complete answer. You can't build a birdhouse in your back yard just by picturing it. It is disappointing to simply try to "attract" a birdhouse. Or to read books on how to "attract" wealth. Deeply disappointing.

But the great thing is this. You wouldn't *want* it to be that simple. Because you would lose the opportunity to participate in its creation. It isn't the birdhouse that gives you joy (ask people who buy things to make them happy). It is the *making of the birdhouse*.

It isn't the masterpiece; it's the act of painting it.

Because when we ourselves are not creating, when we are not doing the doing, when we are not *in the game* actively playing to win, we lose. Then we get testy. We watch others who *are* participating in life and playing game after game and sometimes we even try to live off of them. We imagine that our favorite team is actually us. Or we try to live through our active children. Caution! That can lead to madness.

For example, in today's newspaper it says that a New York man has been charged with beating his mother to death with a barbell after losing his temper while watching a baseball game on television.

Give me a minute to take that in. Now I can see it. It's the watchers who go insane, not the players. This is true in all of life: Fans riot; players are fine. When I went to my son's basketball games it was the parents whose behavior was often rageful, delusional and ugly. They freaked out. They grew furious with the referees or the coaches. It's the watchers that have the problems. It's the passive who go crazy with rage. Smashing pumpkins . . . like the song says . . . despite all my rage I'm still just a rat in a cage.

Fearless means you're not just watching. Not just imagining. Not just picturing and attracting. But you are actually doing things. You're in the game. Fearless means that you yourself are building the birdhouse.

Somebody should tell us . . . right at the
start of our lives . . . that we are dying.
Then we might live to the limit, every
minute of every day. Do it! I say.
Whatever you want to do, do it now!
There are only so many tomorrows.

Michael Landon

Chapter 37

Please just tell us we're dying

Somebody . . . somebody we respect and trust . . . should tell us we're dying. So we'll believe it. That's what Michael Landon said when he got the word from his doctors that he only had a few months to live. Boy did he ever live, then. He really caught the spirit of the precious moment—of making each breath count for something.

Then he thought it was too bad that *all* people didn't realize they were going to die. Didn't all people really realize that? Well . . . maybe . . . but they tried not to think about it. Oh they might admit it was technically true—if they were pressed—but they didn't realize it. They never made it real (never *real*ized it). How much life it would have given them if they had.

Brenda Ueland wrote a book that helped me with my writing more than any other book ever has. It was called *If You Want to Write*. She said it was such a shame when people did not have daily creativity in their lives. She said its lack came from fear. It came from "fear of acting and making mistakes. It is a refusal to follow one's vision. It is a wish to get everybody's approval by being utterly harmless, a zero."

Fear does strange things like that. It can have me *not even living* my life. It can have me, instead, trying to get everyone's approval. Rather than saying no to what I don't want, I say yes. Rather than simplifying my life, I complicate it. Rather than focusing on the best things I can do today, I try to do everything under the sun. Rather than being bold, I try to seem like I'm harmless.

But tell us we are dying and it becomes different. Tell us we are dying and we come alive.

Let your plans be dark and
as impenetrable as night,
and when you move,
fall like a thunderbolt.

Sun Tzu

Chapter 38

Just let the game come to you

My plans used to be huge. I wanted to be Tony Robbins. I watched him flying across the stage doing karate kicks to space odyssey movie music. Then it hit me how exhausted I would be being like him, good as he was. So I soon let my plans become more receptive to the energy of the universe. My mind opened. That felt much better. No big plan. No awakening of the giant within. I would just help whoever asked for help.

I would let the game come to me. I wouldn't force the game. I wouldn't push the river. I wouldn't advertise or promote myself all that much. I would be like Michael Jordan was when he decided to let the game come to him. Stop being a superstar and learn Phil Jackson's triangle offense. It takes a whole team, not just one person, to win a championship. Suddenly there were championships in Jordan's life. He'd go down the court, pass the ball off, and let the game come to him.

Now I am called and then paid to journey all over. The game comes to me. People call and say they are troubled. Their businesses are struggling. Or they need personal, professional coaching. Their careers are stuck. Their relationships are veering off course. Their children are disappointing or disappearing. So I go.

I am mainly a business coach so spouses and children are not supposed to be my specialty, but my clients sometimes insist that it is exactly what's in the way of their career success.

"My wife has grown cold," said a client in hushed tones. "And she's let herself go." I take a moment before I reply. Then I speak.

"She fired herself?"

"No. You know. Physically."

"So your sales are down? Her weight is up and therefore your sales are down?"

This is what I do. Not an easy job. I journey out and help people define their fears. I help them look inside themselves instead of eying the new spousal figure as sport. Because *inside* is where they find the answers. Inside their own layers of fear.

Chapter 39

The whipsaw of mood

One way to begin phasing fear out of *your* life is to start eliminating this antiquated concept known as bad news. Because it's that whipsaw of polarizing mood swings between good news and bad news that sucks all the courage and creativity out of your system.

I read an interesting book that I'd bought when Terry Hill and I did a bookstore walking tour of New York. It was Steven Johnson's *Everything Bad is Good for You*. It's a wonderful book that explains why the human race is getting brighter every day. It's because of (not in spite of) our pop culture of computer games, video games, quiz shows and movies like *Memento*.

He devoted a lot of pages to what he considered to be the forerunner of high-IQ games, APBA Baseball! That was a game Terry and I played a lot as kids so it was great to get confirmation that the very playing of that game boosted our IQs into the stratosphere. I played these games for hours with Terry when we were young. Computers weren't around. We did what we could for mental amusement. Our parents thought the games were bad for us. Baaaad for us! Bad news! Our parents simply didn't know.

Looking back on your life you'll notice that "bad news" wasn't always such bad news. It often—in fact, almost always—turned out to be for the best. Losing one thing creates a vacuum for something better to fill in. It's the way of the universe. Like Leonard Cohen sings, there is a crack in everything. That's how the light gets in.

I was in a company once that suffered a total collapse in the face of violations, lawsuits and more trouble than I'll want to recount. Bad news, right? Everyone was out of a job overnight. Including me! It was horrible.

Or so I thought.

Until I finally looked at what profession I would do next and chose this work I'm doing now—I may never have done this work were it not for that bad news. So today whenever "bad news" arrives I want to turn it over and over before I label it. I want to hold it up to the sun until I can see the gold in it. I owe a lot to bad news in my life. It has always been beneficial.

I can't tell you how many times people, when telling their life stories say, "I was really upset about that at the time but it turned out to be the best thing that ever happened to me." Time turns bad into good. But so does wisdom. The wisdom to know the difference. Here and now. The wisdom to not judge or give events and situations a positive or negative charge. Why keep letting the radio fall into your bathtub?

A fearless life will never depend on the news that comes in today. A fearless life will depend on the gentle spirit already inside you . . . the one that you're relaxing into right now.

Chapter 40

Getting beyond bad and good

One of the guests at a party I attended a year ago asked me what the curriculum focus was at the University of Santa Monica, where I was doing some teaching at the time, and when I said, "Spiritual Psychology," he let out with a yawp, a kind of subhuman braying, a cynical laugh, signifying to me that he was intellectually superior to anything that sounded like "new age" nonsense to him, and that he preferred to take his pessimism STRAIGHT . . . the *New York Times* was all he needed to read to know the psychology of the human species through and through.

I surely don't blame anyone for skepticism, but the irony is that USM is actually *more* intellectually advanced than the old school gray lady psychologies. It not only embraces the best of traditional psychology and incorporates it, but also adds so many more dimensions. These are only termed as "spiritual" because we've run out of words for their depth. And their depth is only known by the profound effects of the work they do.

I myself have participated in all kinds of psychotherapy and groups, and almost any treatment or self-help known to our age, and what distinguishes this school is its effectiveness, and the mood and spirits of its grads. The people I work with there are both brilliant and happy. The *New York Times* says you can't be both. It says that if you're brilliant you're condemned to be a pessimist. A nihilist even. The more you know the worse it gets. So for them it's easier to think of all "new age" as the same laughable thing: crystals, pyramids, channeling, etc. Just as it's easier to think all Republicans, or all Democrats, or all Israelis, or all Mexicans are alike. It's easier to think in labels and categories. It's easier to judge than to understand.

Understanding takes real work. Why not just kill the people we don't understand? Label them first. Demonize them. Then go after them with home made bombs on a mission from God.

This guest at the party with the instant laugh was haunted by the demons of right and wrong. He's made himself into a very limited person by the torment of constantly trying to decide who's good and who's bad.

I have a friend I will call Frank who—no matter when I call him—is either in a good mood (because of good news that has come in) or in a bad mood (because, of course, of the bad news he's just received).

"How are you doing, Frank?"

"Oh, it's *not good* right now."

"What's up?"

"My book got rejected by the one publisher I thought would want it."

"So what's Plan B?"

"Well I didn't have any Plan B because I really had my hopes up for this and it's just going to take a while for me to process the disappointment."

"You're the master, though, Frank. You're so practiced in this."

"The master of what?"

"Disappointment. Taking bad news to heart. Letting things get to you. Savoring injustices."

"Oh, thanks. Your compliments are not like other people's compliments, but thank you."

"Because I'm the only one who knows you don't need standard compliments. You don't need the good news you're always hoping for, either."

"Just what do you think I need?"

"To go back to work. To engage yourself. Serve some people. Get out of all these childish judgments. Take the bib off, jump down from the high chair, and start creating things—like an artist would do."

"What about processing the pain?"

"Just leave that to me."

"You want to process this pain of mine?"

"Better me than you."

On any given day Frank was an emotional mess because of bad and good. His addiction was to labeling and then reacting. Frank was scaring himself every day. The bad and good news was not scaring Frank because it can't. The brain doesn't even work that way. The brain reacts to thoughts, not events. It reacts to perceptions, not situations. The worst thing that can happen to Frank is his own thought about the situation.

He can drop all that if he practices. He can receive news neutrally and work with it, like clay for a sculpture. Like bricks for a house. If he practices. He will now be *using* the news. He can use it without labeling it as bad or good. He can work in a realm of energy that lives beyond bad and good— an inventor's paradise.

Chapter 41

Your monkey mind will cling

All of us are given a number. A certain amount of heartbeats to live. And that's it. An hour from now 4500 of yours will be gone, never to come back to you. And if you indulge a lot of fear, *more* than forty-five hundred will be gone.

So find ways to slow your heart down. You are most courageous when you are in a relaxed state. The eye of the storm is actually the eye of the tiger. Fearless, dreamless peace.

Peace is at the heart of the no-mind warrior.

This inner peace often comes from letting go of what you thought you wanted so badly. I once wanted many years ago—so very badly—a romantic relationship in my life. I was frantic. Dating this person and that. Frustrating myself with my own dream. My little sister Cindy talked to me on the phone one day. She listened to my amorous escapades calmly and said, "It will come to you in good time but you have to stop wanting it. Once you no longer want or need it, there it will be."

She was right. I gave up the anxious mission. Then one day, out of nowhere, there it was.

It arrived because I stopped clinging to the idea that it would bring me happiness. That I needed it. We cling to so much that way. Hopes and dreams born of fear.

All hopes and wishes are born of fear. They are a *clinging* to an imaginary "better" condition than this. Why just hope and dream? Work now. This is all you need. This gentle fearless moment right now.

In Africa, South America and Asia they set traps for monkeys by putting bait—usually delicious nuts—honey nuts! —inside a jar tied to a tree. The opening in the jar is just large enough for the monkey to get his hand in, but when he grasps the nuts, he can't pull his clenched fist out. He can't remove it from the trap without letting go.

When the hunter who wants to catch the monkey approaches, the monkey sees him and goes ape—shrieking, spitting, snarling and hopping all around with his arm still stuck in the jar simply because he refuses to let go. The hunter creeps closer, and the monkey still squirms, still stuck in the jar. The hunter catches him, because even up to the very end the monkey refuses to let go.

What jar is your hand in today?

The cradle rocks above an abyss, and common sense tells us that our existence is but a brief crack of light between two eternities of darkness. Although the two are identical twins, man, as a rule, views the prenatal abyss with more calm than the one he is heading for (at some forty-five hundred heartbeats an hour.)

Vladimir Nabokov
Speak Memory

Chapter 42

Happy to be home from the future

The airplane trip from Phoenix to LA was blissfully spent asleep. It's only an hour anyway, and as I started my usual primordial sound transcendental meditation practice that I always do on take-off I drifted from absence of conscious thought into absence of consciousness itself.

Next thing I knew we had landed in LA and Kathy and I were riding in a taxi to Santa Monica, noticing all the glorious and unusual roadside (oceanside!) California plants and flowers we don't see in Phoenix. At the hotel we had a snack in the outdoor garden Koi Pond restaurant just three feet from the actor Damon Wayans, who was at the table next to us discussing some script about NASCAR. (Not that we were listening in.)

Celebrity is seductive. People's stories are alluring to the ego. We want to eavesdrop. Soon we want to start a story about ourselves. To build it up against the fear. Against the dread that we won't matter. We won't "amount to" anything. We won't *make* it! Ego stories come from the fear that we may never impress anyone. A totally baseless, groundless fear, but it's strong enough to waste a human life.

I'm here in California to do a day-long Saturday seminar called "The Joy of Leadership." A new life for people who didn't know how much fun creative, courageous leadership could be. Can leadership be a joy? Most managers say no. But joy, in my opinion, comes from knowing how to access the higher vibratory states of consciousness: such as humor, creativity, music, laughter, and fearless imagination. Fearless creativity. Keep mixing those factors into your life, and you will not only experience joy, but your team will succeed beyond your wishes. With you in the lead.

We think spirit lives beyond the mind and the body. Out there in some "better" realm than this one. So now we have to call on it. Or pray for it. Or earn it. We desperately "call on the light" not knowing we *are* light. Isn't spirit already always infusing both mind and body with the life force? But still we "reach out" calling for the light . . . we are like the sun asking to borrow a candle.

Shallow, flatland reductionist psychology lets you study your childhood and adolescent history of wounds and negative beliefs, but that's all. One of the reasons that skillful life coaches sometimes succeed where psychologists have failed is because of a life coach's effectively enthusiastic approach to finding his client's strength in the moment. Right now. Simply *dropping* the past as we skip ahead! Let's create a quickening in your life! As the great poet Rilke said, and I know I'm repeating this, "The future enters into us, to be transformed in us, long before it happens." (The best psychotherapist of our age, Nathaniel Branden, has now added life coaching to his list of services for those who are willing to move on.)

To prepare for presenting this leadership course Kathy and I took long walks by the beach and through the California streets as the Pacific Ocean air curled her hair. Einstein said there was only one question we humans needed to have answered for us, and that is whether or not the universe was kind. By its very nature. And maybe if I were as enlightened as Gandhi or St. Francis or Kathy I would already be seeing the underlying kindness at every turn.

But I'm not so gifted. Or practiced. That's a better word. I'm not there yet anyway. Not yet. I often brood internally, missing the beauty that surrounds me. That's why it's good to have Kathy with me, a constant connoisseur of the visible wonders before us on this green and sometimes blue planet. She points out the pelicans flying toward the pier in Santa Monica over the ocean in astonishing formation as we lay in the sand. I am not noticing. Instead I'm listening to the rhythmic drumbeat of the waves making counterpoint to my internal mood. What if I'm not good enough tomorrow? I think back to my teenage years, back to the poet Vachel Lindsay and my classmates and me reading aloud in high school, over and over, in booming voices: *Then I heard the boom of the blood-lust song / And a thigh-bone beating on a tin-pan gong.*

My blood pounds as I brood about the course I'm giving tomorrow. My mantra on that day will be E.M. Forster's quote, "Only connect." I've written more books than E.M. Forster and J.D. Salinger combined, but not yet a one as good as any of theirs. Pick their worst. Pick my best. Theirs still win! There may be time, though. Still. I hope. As the waves roll in and the waves roll out. I feel the boom. The ego builds its hopeless sandcastle. Maybe I'll be as good as Salinger. Hopeless. Desperate, even. Sand. Made of sand, this imagined life! This yearning for recognition.

Kathy tries again. This time she physically takes my face in her hands and turns my head so I can see the soaring birds above the oceanside pier. I am startled, and take an involuntary deep breath. Then I take another breath. I am back on earth. Breathing deeply. All ego falls aside. The beauty of the birds in flight surprises me. I am here. I am now. There is no tomorrow any more, and because I have returned from the future, there is no more fear.

Whenever we split seamless awareness into a subject versus an object, into a self versus an other, then that self feels fear, simply because there are now so many "others" out there that can harm it.

Ken Wilber

Chapter 43

It's time to break my mind

I went to a twelve-step meeting the other day to spiritualize my mind. In the meeting a man with 15 years of sobriety said that life still sometimes gave him problems. He said, "Even though the monkey's off my back the circus is still in town." I looked at him and smiled. I thought about the song "Paper Moon" after he said that. In that song there's a line about this circus of a world we live in that says, "It's a Barnum and Bailey world, just as phony as it can be."

I'll be doing a lot of business traveling throughout this Barnum and Bailey world in the coming weeks. The circus is definitely in town. Because look how fear shows up unexpectedly, riding in on the back of the elephant. Look how fear causes me to lie.

First the fear, then the lie. Because I feel a little like I'm doing a Tour de France I think about a bike race I read about called the Vuelta a Espana. The American cyclist Tyler Hamilton tried so hard to explain how someone else's blood had found its way into his veins during that bike race in 2004. (He was apparently cheating with transfusions.) First fear, then the lie: Hamilton argued that he was a chimera—someone with two types of blood, the result of having shared his mother's womb with a vanished twin.

Wow. I compare that one to all the lies I've told and I really feel dull and unimaginative. So I'm saying it isn't the cheating itself that fascinates us so much as do the amazing stories and explanations. Fear results from the belief that you're going to lose something. That you might even lose the Vuelta a Espana!

To stop that mental two-step: first the fear, then the lie— I had to learn to break the pattern. In a way, to break my mind.

George Hamilton IV had a song back in the 50s that I always liked called *Break My Mind*. It was also later sung by Linda Ronstadt and more than 20 other recording artists. I love it because it captures the image of how we freeze ourselves with our scary beliefs. Those beliefs crystallize and the mind becomes like a sheet of ice.

I remember growing up in Michigan and after a freezing rain you could lift sheets of ice, about the size of record album covers, up from the sidewalk. They were translucent and crystalline. You would hold them in wonder, then fling them against a Maple tree and shatter them. That's how our minds get! Our minds are like ice when we freeze with fear. Like a picture frame full of ice. Frozen. I can feel it.

That's when I know I need to break my mind.

Music can break my mind because the vibrations are so powerful. They shake my nerves and they rattle my brain. How marvelous to get untracked this way. What a glorious wake-up call to clarity. Break my mind! Soon I'm thinking of this lyric by the Grateful Dead: "The bus came by and I got on, that's when it all began. There was Cowboy Neal at the wheel of the bus to Never-ever-land."

The song was called "The Other One," and that Neal at the wheel was Neal Cassady, whom Allen Ginsburg called the secret hero of his poems and who inspired *On The Road* by Jack Kerouac. Kerouac and Cassady were drunks who had "Creative Writers" as their cover stories. Because writing takes such discipline (to access the subconscious, creative mind) most writers would rather drink than write because it seems to work faster. Have a few drinks and you feel creative. Now they can hang out with other "writers" who drink and hope they are *living* their unwritten novels.

I tried that approach myself! Why not just get drunk and LIVE your novel?!? Seemed easier. But it never delivered. Laziness turns out to be hell itself. The lazy mind must be broken.

My best mind break occurred when I went into a recovery program and found out there were three things in life, not just two. I found out that there was more to life than just the mind and the body. There was also spirit. Beautiful, fearless spirit.

If we are going to insist on identifying with just the little self in here, then others are going to bruise it, insult it, injure it. The ego, then, is kept in existence by a collection of emotional insults; it carries its personal bruises as the fabric of its very existence. It actively collects hurts and insults, even while resenting them, because without its bruises it would be, literally, nothing.

Ken Wilber

Chapter 44

Pour me a way to fly home

An interviewer once asked Vladimir Nabokov, "What are your views about man's upward climb from slime?" and Nabokov replied, "A truly remarkable performance. A pity, though, that some of the slime still sticks to drugged brains."

Addiction offers a *simulation* of conscious contact with a higher power. But the problem is that it is a simulation, not the real thing. Like getting in a flight simulator and trying to fly it somewhere.

So picture yourself on an air force base when they have flight simulators where people learn to fly. And all of a sudden a nuclear bomb hits the base! You have to get out of town, fast! So you climb into the flight simulator and fire it up! But you don't really go anywhere. Because it's only a simulator. Like alcohol itself. Like drugs. *Simulators* are all they are. Imitations of life. You don't really charm anyone. You are not really the life of the party, as you imagine you are. And if you're not sure about this, let me play the tape— or let me show you the video of you in your simulator, thinking, *thinking* you are flying across the country. Pathetic. William Blake said a fool who persists in his folly will become wise. Or dead. Same thing? Maybe it's the same thing. Woody Allen suggests it is. He said, "Death is God's way of telling you to slow down."

Addicts (like I was) talk about hitting bottom. But where is bottom? First gear? Second? One man's bottom is another man's high. Thank God for the shift that the mind can make . . . all the way up to the courage to change the things I can.

I have met on the street a very poor man who was in love. His hat was old, his coat was out at the elbows, the water passed through his shoes, and the stars through his soul.

Victor Hugo

Chapter 45

The fearless life sparkles with light

It's funny that when my mind is full of worry it sees the world as threatening. This mood sees everything wrong with the world. But when I'm refreshed and illumined from the inside, I start seeing how good people are to each other. How everyone wants to help everyone else. It's what a fresh, clear mind will see.

Polish the glass, and you'll see even more. A lot of people thought that J.D. Salinger's great character in fiction, Seymour Glass, was named because of that idea. "See more glass." He was a seer, a poet and a modern day saint. When I was young and reading Salinger I used to wish more people were like that. Back then I thought people had permanent personalities and finite characters and they were either like Seymour or they weren't.

What I'm glad I've learned since then is that *we can all* see like that and be like that. We can all polish the glass and see more. In this moment right here. We can all have the illumined fearless mind that Emerson speaks of.

But first the dull mind has to have shifted. Which was Emerson's point when he said, "To the dull mind all nature is leaden. To the illumined mind the whole world burns and sparkles with light." And what he was talking about is the fearless mind; the same one possessed absolutely for sure and for certain by everyone.

People travel to wonder at the height of
the mountains, at the huge waves of the
seas, at the long course of the rivers,
at the vast compass of the ocean,
at the circular motion of the stars,
and yet they pass by themselves
without wondering.

St. Augustine

Chapter 46

This little light of mine

I had a friend who no matter what challenge he was facing would always email all his friends and beg them to "send light."

"I'm about to take my real estate exam, send light!" "My cat has an operation today, send light!" "The IRS is auditing me, send light!" "My car has a faulty fuel pump, send light!" "My son's applying to college, send light!"

"Why do you need all this light?" I asked him.

"It always helps to have light sent to you," he said.

"And how would it feel not to need light?"

"That would be awesome."

"And how can you be sure you don't already have enough light?"

"I can feel that I don't. I'm worried about too many things."

If my friend were a character in *Dances with Wolves* his name would be Not Enough Light.

I got a call from Not Enough Light the other day and he told me he was going through a difficult separation from his girlfriend.

"How can I help you with this?" I asked him.

"Send me light," he said.

"Oh, for crying out loud," I said, "Why don't we just talk in person? Let me come see you."

I flew up to see my friend. I wanted Not Enough Light to know that he *was* the light. In fact, he was made of stars. Not only was that true metaphorically, but it was true scientifically. Scientists have proven that the same elements that make up the stars in the galaxies are also what *we* are made of!

Humans (and most things biological) are made mostly of carbon, hydrogen, oxygen and nitrogen. The same thing stars are made of. Sometime, somewhere, a star exploded and the little quantum nano-bits got blasted away into showers of light particles that came to be you and me.

Tinker Bell had a version of this going on that she called pixie dust. She could sprinkle it on another person. Send dust! As if that person needed it. But our fairy tales rise up as stories to deal with fear. Peter Pan was a beautiful, colorful embodiment of "I won't grow up! I don't want to be a man!" Why not? Because it looks frightening. But what Peter didn't know was that he had nothing to worry about. He was made of light.

We are all of us failures—at least,
the best of us are.

James Barrie

Chapter 47

What will you do with your life?

W hat would you do if you could not possibly fail? If failure were not even a possibility, what would you do with your life right now?

I love asking those questions because it unconceals and reveals our cowering-under-the-covers fear of failure. Yes, fear of failure is the culprit that is stopping us from having a fearless, adventurous life. Fear of failure! It's everywhere.

James Barrie, who wrote the Peter Pan stories, has hit on something, however. He has now said that we are all failures . . . at least the best of us are.

He has linked failure to being the best. And what this uncovers is that people who are *not* failures are people who have never gone too far . . . which is to say they have never gone far enough. You'll never know how far you can go unless you are willing to go too far. That alone will tell you. These people who never go too far are people who have always kept it safe . . . who have figured out how to exist within the narrow confines of their limitations and then just hang there. Safe.

Failure suggests that you flew into something unknown to you and got rudely rejected.

Like Elvis was rejected by the Grand Ole Opry who, at first, told him to give up this singing career because he was just too weird for country. That wasn't his only failure. Elvis also failed early in his career to make an impact in Las Vegas. Too odd for Vegas! Vegas was used to the ring-a-ding-ding glitz of the rat pack crowd, and when he first went there Elvis was a down and dirty rockabilly boy. Boooo! Get him off! We want real entertainment! Remove that failure!

One of the wonderful things about failing is that you can re-gather yourself, pick yourself up, dust yourself off and proceed. Now you know more. Now you're wiser and stronger. And now you are losing your fear of failure because you know you can dance with it! It doesn't have to stop you!

James Barrie identifies a deeply profound mind shift when he says, "We are all of us failures—at least, the best of us are." It's a tectonic shift to think the best of us fail and the worst of us have *never failed at anything.*

The music teacher came twice each week to bridge the awful gap between Dorothy and Chopin.

George Ade

Chapter 48

This is who you might have been

George Ade was a beloved humorist, journalist and a writer of plays and fables. His quote on the previous page is funny, but it also identifies something important: the gap! The awful gap between Dorothy and Chopin.

That fearful gap is seen everywhere by all of us.

It's the gap between what is, and what we think would be better. You'll find the source of fear in this gap. But we wake up from fearing the gap when we hear that the great writer George Eliot said, "It's never too late to be who you might have been." It's never too late. And she knew. It wasn't a theory to her. She? Her? George was a she? Yes, because there was a gap in her life, too, which led her to take on the role of a man! George was really Mary! Mary Anne Evans. She knew she could write like the dickens, even like *the* Dickens. But in her times women were not thought to be capable of being novelists so she bridged the gap by taking on the name of a fictional man, George Eliot, for the purpose of her books. As Eliot she wrote the classic novels, *Middlemarch, Silas Marner* and *Daniel Deronda*.

How do I close the gap between who I am and who I want to be?

The courage to do that comes from releasing a thought. Whatever the thought is that is producing the fear. Here's the irony of the awful gap: you'll leave a place faster when it's okay that you're there. Lose the fear of where you are and you are more free than ever to go to where you might have been.

Chapter 49

Yes, you can find Waldo

Angie was worried about not having a job. She was divorced and taking care of a daughter with cancer and she called to ask me how to lose the fear of not finding work.

We talked for a long time about how qualified she was. I told her how avidly organizations were searching for good people. And I told Angie how this amazed me. As a coach to small businesses (and many not so small) I have never *ever* seen one that wouldn't love an Angie. Dedicated, coachable, upbeat, smart, energetic and friendly. Who wouldn't want that?

And nearly every leader I've ever worked with would say, "How do you find a person like *that*?"

Leaders are fraught with the frustrations of going to online help wanted services, using the newspaper in vain, and often ending up with "head cases" working for them—unhappy people who drag their personal issues into work with them every day. Complainers. Malcontents. Professional whiners.

Where's Angie? Where do I find her?

And yet I also experience the other side. The Angies, who are such great people—either stuck in jobs that are bad fits for them, or out of work, or just entering the job market, worried. Worried that there is nothing there for them.

So when I say to Angie, "What you are seeking is seeking you," she thinks I'm not connected to the real world . . . that I'm going spiritual on her at the worst possible time.

"In one month I am going to begin my search," she says.

"Wonderful. The world will be glad you're searching."

"Really?"

"And remember to base your search on what *you* would love to do."

"That would be nice. And it feels good to put it on the calendar for 30 days from now so I know it's definite."

"That's good," I said. "And in the meantime, during those 30 days when you're getting your affairs in order, don't forget to stay open."

"Stay what?"

"Stay open."

I wanted Angie to be open to opportunity that would be peeking in at her *now* . . . now that she had a clear intention to find work.

She was skeptical about that idea, saying, "Oh, like the law of attraction? Picture what you want and it will just show up?"

"Yes, but it's not that mystical."

She looked confused so I decided to say it in a different way.

"Ask yourself this: Where's Waldo?" I said.

"Where's who?"

"Where's Waldo?"

"You mean like those kids' puzzles? Where there's this huge scene and you have to find Waldo hidden in there somewhere?"

"Exactly."

"How does that relate to my finding a job?"

I told Angie that if I'd just handed her that big picture to look at with no mention of a Waldo she'd *never* see Waldo in there because she wasn't looking for him. But the minute she started looking at the picture with Waldo *in her mind*, she upped the chances of finding him by a thousand percent.

It would be the same in her job hunt. The minute she started looking at the whole world with a new job *in mind* she would see a lot of surprising coincidences. She would open herself to the possibility that what she was seeking was seeking her. She'd notice things she didn't notice before. She would hear things in conversations she wouldn't have heard before. That email from her friend crowing about starting her exciting new company would be read with different eyes.

So what's missing? Angie would love a good job and employers would love Angie. What's missing?

The courage to connect. From both sides. Because unless both sides become fearless in their quest, both sides of the equation will never know about each other. Neither will reach out to the other to create the bridge that will carry them across the river of fear and ignorance. The employer's fear that there aren't good people eager to work for him causes him to not reach out very enthusiastically or creatively. He will not *love* recruiting and hiring.

And the same could happen with Angie. Too afraid that "there's nothing out there," she will limit her search to the most obvious possibilities. She, too, does not *love* the job search.

What I'd wish for Angie and her potential employer is an awakening to the link between love and success. Love and fear are the opposites in life, not love and hate. If we saw this we would conquer fear with love. We would take something on with so much enthusiasm that we'd love it (we tend to love what we devote ourselves to in a big way and practice until we're good at it.)

Love is always creative. Fear is always destructive. So love, therefore, is the answer to fear, because love creates. Love creates the courage . . . to change . . . the things you can.

Chapter 50

It's a wonder we can think at all

"When I think *back* on all the *crap* I learned in high school," sings Paul Simon, "it's a wonder I can think at all."

One thing I noticed about my own children's schools was that there wasn't a lot of emphasis put on teaching children to be fearless. Or even to succeed. Which classes taught that? To set bold goals and create success?

(One exception to that were the teachers who coached sports. Somehow they knew its importance. But they were the exceptions.)

I visited one of my children's schools once to give a talk on goal achievement. I chatted with the principal of the school before going into the class to talk to the kids. I asked the principal, "How much time do these kids spend on this subject?"

"What subject do you mean?"

"Setting goals . . . learning to get the life you want."

"That's hardly a subject of academic pursuit."

"Okay, succeeding. Career mastery. How much time on that?"

"Well . . . none . . . "

"So, of all the thousands of hours of a child's education in your school system *not one* of those hours is spent on how to get the life they want?"

"I'm afraid I'm not following you here. I am sure, though, if there were an important subject in what you are talking about we'd be teaching it."

I didn't try to argue further. To the schools, the kids getting the life they wanted wasn't important. I thanked the principal for the opportunity to talk to one of her classes about fearless success, and I had an enjoyable time doing so. Children are so eager for this subject.

Bitterness is the underlying theme at schools. Bitterness about the opportunities of life. Kids emerge from school trying to get jobs with companies they've been taught to think of as greed-based. Or they might be trying to make a profit in their own small businesses after having been taught that the "profit-motive" is an embarrassing motive for anything. So their little companies don't make a profit. (It's hard to be masterful at something you are ashamed of.) Soon they go out of business. It's a wonder they can think at all.

And while it's true that we need to study our Enrons, and put the egomaniacal charlatans who run scams like that into jail, it is *not* a service to the next generation to condemn the entire free market. And to not teach a way to participate freely in a system that benefits all when executed with integrity.

Why do we want to make people afraid? Why, especially, do we make our own children afraid? Why make them afraid of the one thing that will set them free? A fearless life will always be hard for them until we decide to change this.

Happiness is permanent. It is
always there.
What comes and goes is unhappiness.
If you identify with what comes and
goes, you will be unhappy.
If you identify with what is permanent
and always there, you are
happiness itself.

Poonjaji

Chapter 51

What we can learn from Star Trek

While on a plane flying into New York I read in *Esquire* magazine a little piece called "What I've Learned" . . . an interview with *Star Trek*'s William Shatner! In it Shatner says that this is what he's learned from life: "You have to create your life. You have to carve it, like a sculpture." And he also says (and I underlined this one with my pen), "We meet aliens every day who have something to give us. They come in the form of people with different opinions."

William Shatner realized that he had become kind of a joke in the public eye after his time as Captain Kirk on *Star Trek* had ended. He didn't have a lot of acting talent, and his public personality was awkward and clumsy. He didn't know how to go on talk shows and sound witty and smart.

But he decided, after a long while, to stop *reacting* to that situation. He looked at the situation and accepted it. (Acceptance is fearless.) He decided he would just *go with it*. If the public thought he was a kind of buffoon and a has-been, then that was fine with him; he would be that for them. He was soon playing a buffoon and a has-been called Denny Crane in *Boston Legal*. He was brilliant at it. He was funny. He won an Emmy! He was no longer a has-been! *Esquire* magazine sought him out for an interview. And look! In his interview he was witty and smart!

And his conclusion about all of it was so accurate. To be happy? You have to create your life. You have to carve it, like a sculpture. And when he did that his life shifted from miserable to fearless.

Nothing outside you
can ever give you
what you're looking for.

Byron Katie

Chapter 52

Don't put the butterfly back in

So much fear comes from our story. The story of me. The story of you. We are afraid something will happen to our story! It's a story we have spun like a cocoon over the years to keep us safe from other people's criticism.

We feel we have to spin this story . . . and the silky embellishments we add to it. The threads of embellishment wrap a cocoon around the butterfly of spirit we were born with. We force the butterfly back into the cocoon! By wrapping it with this silky spin.

When someone refuses this path, it's inspiring to see. Like that guy we saw dancing on TV last night. A grown man dancing! Doesn't he look a lot like Mark Cuban? Whatever you think of Mark Cuban, the multimillionaire owner of the Dallas Mavericks—one thing you can't deny is that he challenges fear. He is not content to just live off the silk of his story.

He decided to challenge fear again when he became a contestant on *Dancing with the Stars*. I had great fun watching him!

Cuban said he got up every morning no matter how sore he was to work on his dance routines, sometimes for six hours! For six hours. If you had his millions would you do that? Why did he do that? He lost 30 pounds in the process. But really.

"What it reminded me more of than anything was the feeling of being a kid and moving to a new neighborhood," said Mark Cuban. "The fear, the excitement, the uncertainty, the newness of it all. Not knowing if I was going to be picked first or last for the game and whether or not I would live up to either. Knowing that feeling again. That's a win."

Knowing that fear again. That's a win. That's a paradox! There is a connection we might see between his astonishing career success and always wanting to know that feeling again. How courage is rewarded. God grant me! Courage like that.

A young and revered folk icon Bob Dylan once challenged his own story. He walked out on the Newport Folk Festival stage and plugged in his electric guitar and transformed himself from Woody Guthrie to a rock singer in the face of a crowd that booed him for selling out. *Boo! Boooo, Dylan, you sellout!*

But he played on. He kept going in the face of the boos. Like a rolling stone. No direction home. Fearless.

What are we cocoons so afraid of? What do we cocoons think will happen if we plug our guitars in and just play?

Actually take a minute now to identify and capture on paper what you are afraid would happen. If you dropped everything and did the life you wanted to. Have you written the fear down? Now look at it. Now list the other fears you have. Write them down too. Now sit back and look at them all. Notice something about them. They are all in the future. Aren't they? All fears are a trembling mental projection into an absolutely non-existent future.

So if all fear is in the future, then we can simply take our action *out* of the future. We can merely come back home. Bring ourselves into the present moment. Plugging the guitar right in right now.

You will notice something. When you plugged in to the present moment—when you're right here loving and thriving in the now—there's no more worry or anger. Some would use the word fearless to describe how that feels.

My freedom will be so much the greater and more meaningful the more narrowly I limit my field of action and the more I surround myself with obstacles. Whatever diminishes constraint diminishes strength. The more constraints one imposes, the more one frees one's self of the chains that shackle the spirit.

Igor Stravinsky
Poetics of Music

Chapter 53

Who will really inherit the earth?

My friend Lindsay Brady is a master of the gentle discipline known as hypnotherapy. He alters lives by altering perceptions—if you can now *perceive* yourself as a non-smoker—at the deep level of identity and being—you simply won't smoke anymore—because non-smokers just don't. It's all in your perception. Who *are* you?

Joni Mitchell has been smoking since she was nine. Afraid to quit. (I watched an interview with her recently in which she said she suffers daily ongoing sadness from what is happening to the planet. The pollution. She almost can't bear it.) She is so talented a songwriter. I play her music all the time. And she chain-smokes . . . she smokes on stage, in art museums, and even in the face of a doctor showing her fiber optic shots of an open wound on her larynx.

I know what it's like to be like that. Afraid to quit. Afraid to get help. Not being able to perceive handling life without something. I was once afraid I wouldn't be able to handle the absence of addictive substance. So I know.

Addiction and fear are strange bedfellows. Their relationship to each other is toxic but warm. They fuel and feed each other relentlessly. And it's all perception. The *Independent* newspaper in Britain said, "Joni Mitchell chain-smokes, and it's one of the smoothest chains you've ever seen. As her left hand stubs one out, her right is already loosening the next from the packet." Life without that chain seems unthinkable to the fear that even ignores an open wound in the larynx.

Lindsay Brady taught me how to use the mind to program the brain. The mind sends a crisp color photo to the brain—a photo of what I want. It's a clear perception. (Healthy lungs, free breathing, long life.) There are neurological pathways in the human brain that now accept that picture. I program these pathways by choice. These paths and patterns are now formed through repetition of picture-forming words.

Most people have this process backward, and that is precisely where their fear comes from. They picture what they *dread*! They picture what they hope won't happen. Worst-case scenarios are fed into the fax machine of the brain. Fear! Soon the brain is even looking, yes, *looking* for signs of manifestation of that fear. Combing the universe for signs of unhappy life.

For example, if the brain fears that a relationship will go bad, it then interprets even the most innocent, neutral remark as a threat.

"She didn't have to insult me. She could have just trusted me."

"How did she insult you?"

"By saying what she did."

"She just asked you how you were doing."

Some feel that fear is okay as a lifestyle because they've heard that the meek shall inherit the earth. So they can go on with being meek as a way of life. They become soft-spoken and compliant, never standing for themselves; always resigned to being a fluffy doormat.

But scholars now say that in the scriptural texts that were translated from the Greek, the word *praos* doesn't exactly mean "meek" as people have always thought. In fact it is more accurate to say it means "disciplined." A very big difference in those translations. It's much more encouraging to now realize that the disciplined shall inherit the earth.

Chapter 54

Doctor, my eyes have seen the light

The great novelist Marcel Proust said, "The only real voyage of discovery consists not in seeking new landscapes but in having new eyes."

What is my own voyage of discovery? I've finally realized that I can go in or go out. Go *out* and you can only go out so far. You can go to Africa, or even Siam. Faraway places with strange-sounding names. Some humans have actually gone to the moon.

But when they come back, what's next? Isn't all travel just there and back? I'm off and back . . . to Letdown Town.

Go *in*, though, and it's infinite. That's a true shift, to shift from the outer discovery to the inner. To have new eyes. Why is that so hard to do? Why do people not trust going in? Do they wonder what's there? But that's the point, you don't know.

What if you sat in a quiet chair in a quiet room all day? What would you experience? Most people wouldn't do that for all the money in the world. So addicted they are to external stimulus. No trust for the kingdom of heaven that's within.

But! But "anything that has real and lasting value is always a gift from within," said Franz Kafka. "You don't need to leave your room. Remain sitting at your table and listen. Do not even listen. Simply wait, be quiet, still and solitary. The world will freely offer itself to you to be unmasked, it has no choice, it will roll in ecstasy at your feet."

The problem with people who have not learned to allow this mind shift (the shift is from the deck chairs outside to the gift within) is that they're too busy . . . racing around trying to fix what's outside them all day. Trying to alter the external troubles, giving in to the false impression that the outside is all there is.

Yet now here comes along the famed philosopher Blaise Pascal who is saying, "All people's troubles are caused by one single thing, which is their inability to sit quietly in a room."

So what happens for people who acquire that rare ability? What happens when they sit quietly in a room? What occurs when there's no external input to their brain? Nothing but maybe the birds at the window, or the wind in the willow tree. What happens?

The mind settles down. The mind settles down and begins to reorder itself into a state of harmony and sparkling grace. True power begins to gather. Clarity rings like a crystal glass tapped by a finger. A subtle shift occurs. Fear exits the system.

There is one thing in this world you must never forget to do. Human beings come into this world to do particular work. That work is their purpose, and each is specific to the person. If you forget everything else and not this, there's nothing to worry about. If you remember everything else and forget your true work, then you will have done nothing with your life.

Rumi

Chapter 55

All our fears are optical illusions

A *fata morgana* (Italian translation of Morgan Le Fay, the fairy shape-shifting half sister of King Arthur) is a mirage. It's an optical illusion that results from temperature inversion.

Objects on the horizon (follow this, please, as it relates to everything out there on the horizon known as your future, your fear) . . . objects like ships, cliffs, islands and icebergs look distorted, elongated and elevated.

The mind does that, too. It inverts itself, making life's circumstances look distorted, elongated and elevated. Because all my fears are optical illusions. Therefore, all my trials will soon be over.

Follow this: warm air drifts in over cold air close to the cold ground. The interface of warm and cold creates a kind of refracting lens that inverts images and displays these shimmering fata morgana. Shifting shapes! Fears!

Fata morgana are usually seen in the morning after a cold night. After a cold dark night of the soul. Soon heat has radiated into a cold space and for men at sea it's as if they had taken acid.

Just as hot tempers flow over the cold ground of fear. Anxiety for the morrow sets into your day. And the next thing you know you think you are being tormented by the shape-shifting half sister of King Arthur. You think she is against you.

But in truth? In absolute reality? She loves you more than you know. And more than you *can* know.

Chapter 56

The secret is that you are a sculptor

Sometimes the secret of life comes down to bold, creative moves. In the mind and in the world. And maybe a truly fearless life doesn't take a lot of accumulated wisdom.

It might simply be reflected in what Southwest Airlines' brilliant founder Herb Kelleher used to say: "Yes, we have a 'strategic plan.' It's called 'doing things.'"

I loved what the famous sculptor Henry Moore said about this subject to the poet Donald Hall in Hall's book *Life Work*. Hall had asked Moore—now that Moore had just turned 80—what the secret of life was.

Moore said, "The secret of life is to have a task, something you devote your entire life to, something you bring everything to, every minute of the day for your whole life. And the most important thing is—it must be something you cannot possibly do!"

Moore's task was to be the greatest sculptor who ever lived and to know it.

Most people would think that was a bit obsessive. Most people would scoff at that kind of goal. But I must be different than most people. Because when I came to that part of Hall's book I was lit up for days! I loved it! Because whenever I read something bold like that I suddenly know what I want to do with my life, too.

Courage inspires . . . even the courage of a fearless, impossible vision.

I'm not going to say what my task is, because, for me, talking about it takes energy away from the actual doing of it. Suffice it to say that I am doing it right now.

As a man's real power grows
and his knowledge widens,
ever the way he can follow grows
narrower: until at last he chooses
nothing,
but does only and wholly
what he must do.

Ursula le Guin
A Wizard of Earthsea

About the Author

Contact the author at www.stevechandler.com

Steve Chandler is one of America's best-selling authors whose 16 books have been translated into more than 20 languages throughout Europe, China, Japan, the Middle East and Latin America.

Chandler is also a world-famous public speaker who was called by Fred Knipe, a four-time Emmy-award winning PBS screenwriter, "an insane combination of Anthony Robbins and Jerry Seinfeld." He recently starred in an episode of NBC's *Starting Over*, the Emmy-award winning reality show about life-coaching.

Chandler was recently a guest lecturer at the University of Santa Monica where he taught in the graduate program of Soul-Centered Leadership.

Chandler's first audiobook, *100 Ways to Motivate Yourself*, was named *Chicago Tribune*'s Audiobook of the Year in 1997. *King Features Syndicate* repeated the honor by naming Chandler's *35 Ways to Create Great Relationships* the 1999 Audiobook of the Year.

Chandler has been a trainer and consultant to more than 30 Fortune 500 companies worldwide. He graduated from the University of Arizona with a degree in Creative Writing and Political Science, and spent four years in the U.S. Army in Language and Psychological Warfare. His internationally popular blog is available for all to read at www.stevechandler.com.

A message from Steve Chandler about learning to mind shift

Do not follow the path
Go where there is no path
to begin the trail.

ASHANTI PROVERB

Dear Fellow Traveler,
Fear closes the human mind. It shuts it down. Soon the mind is contracted and shivering in the corner. But when you open your mind to the soft upward spiral of repeated shifts, it soars. And soon what you wanted to "succeed at" becomes a joke . . . it's so easy to do. That's been my experience, anyway. And so on a series of ten CDs called *MindShift* I share it with you.

All my life I waited for this moment: the chance to say that I no longer need to coach you or train you or write a book for you, because it's all contained here: in this new program that teaches you to MIND SHIFT.

It took me 10 CDs to say to you what I wanted to say about success and how to achieve what you want to achieve. How to shift upward from fear to grace and courage and pure action. It's a shift that anyone can do, because it's a shift that happens in the mind.

What if fear were the only real problem you had? Well, it is. And what if a series of shifts in your mind could take you above all that so that you could achieve what you always wanted to achieve?

So listen to these CDs and allow them to become a part of who you are. Play them over and over and don't get too literal or linear about what you are "learning," but just let your mind roam freely while you listen. I've recorded them slowly in a very low-key way so that you can listen again and again and let your mind drift in and out of the content. Soon it will be yours.

What would the ultimate success course have in it? That's what I wondered as I went through the years sampling success courses by all the motivational greats and the new age gurus. Then one day I thought, why don't I just turn on the microphone and say what it is?

Of all the books I've written, of all the audios I've made, this is what I would leave behind. If I could just leave behind one thing for my children and their children and you and your children it would be this. It would be Mind Shift, because it's the only thing that says what I really wanted to say. A mind that is open will shift.

Go here to order it www.stevechandler.com.

Also by Steve Chandler

The Joy of Selling

10 Commitments to Your Success

100 Ways to Create Wealth
(with Sam Beckford)

The Small Business Millionaire
(with Sam Beckford)

RelationShift: Revolutionary Fundraising
(with Michael Bassoff)

Two Guys Read Moby-Dick
(with Terrence N. Hill)

Two Guys Read the Obituaries
(with Terrence N. Hill)

Two Guys Read Jane Austen
(with Terrence N. Hill)

ROBERT D. REED PUBLISHERS ORDER FORM

Call in your order for fast service and quantity discounts

(541) 347- 9882

OR order on-line at **www.rdrpublishers.com** *using PayPal.*
OR order by mail: Make a copy of this form; enclose payment information:

Robert D. Reed Publishers
1380 Face Rock Drive, Bandon, OR 97411

Note: Shipping is $3.50 1st book + $1 for each additional book.

Send indicated books to:

Name _____

Address _____

City _____State _____Zip _____

Phone _____Fax _____Cell _____

E-Mail _____

Payment by check /__/ or credit card /__/ *(All major credit cards are accepted.)*

Name on card _____

Card Number _____

Exp. Date _____Last 3-Digit number on back of card _____

		Qty.
Fearless		
by Steve Chandler $12.95		_____
The Joy of Selling		
by Steve Chandler $11.95		_____
100 Ways to Create Wealth		
by Steve Chandler & Sam Beckford $24.95		_____
Ten Commitments to Your Success		
by Steve Chandler $11.95		_____
Two Guys Read Moby-Dick		
by Steve Chandler & Terrence N. Hill $9.95		_____
Two Guys Read the Obituaries		
by Steve Chandler & Terrence N. Hill $14.95		_____

Other book title(s) from www.rdrpublishers.com:

_____ $ _____

_____ $ _____